ADVANCED GOLF

Steps to Success

DeDe Owens, EdD
Teaching Professional
Cog Hill Golf and Country Club
Lemont, Illinois

Linda K. Bunker, PhD
Sport Psychologist
University of Virginia
Charlottesville, Virginia

Leisure Press
Champaign, Illinois

Library of Congress Cataloging-in-Publication Data

Owens, DeDe
    Advanced golf : steps to success / DeDe Owens, Linda K. Bunker.
        p.   cm.
    Includes bibliographical references.
    ISBN 0-88011-464-9
    1. Golf. I. Bunker, Linda K.   II. Title.
    GV965.086 1992   92-5940
    796.352'3--dc20   CIP

ISBN: 0-88011-464-9

Acquisitions Editor: Brian Holding
Developmental Editor: Judy Patterson Wright, PhD
Assistant Editors: Laura Bofinger, Moyra Knight, and Julie Swadener
Copyeditors: Molly Bentsen and Wendy Nelson
Proofreader: Pam Johnson
Production Director: Ernie Noa
Typesetters: Julie Overholt, Ruby Zimmerman, and Kathy Boudreau-Fuoss
Text Design: Keith Blomberg
Text Layout: Tara Welsch, Denise Lowry, Kimberlie Henris
Cover Design: Jack Davis
Cover Photo: Bill Morrow
Line Drawings and Course Diagrams: Tim Offenstein
Printer: United Graphics, Inc.

Instructional Designer for the Steps to Success Activity Series: Joan N. Vickers, EdD, University of Calgary, Calgary, Alberta, Canada

Some line drawings in Steps 1, 2, 3, and the appendix are from *Coaching Golf Effectively* by D. Owens and L.K. Bunker, 1989, Champaign, Illinois: Human Kinetics Publishers. Copyright 1989 by DeDe Owens and Linda K. Bunker. Reprinted by permission.

Some line drawings in Steps 1, 4, 5, 12, 13, and the appendix are from *Golf Steps to Success* by D. Owens and L.K. Bunker, 1989, Champaign, Illinois: Human Kinetics Publishers. Copyright 1989 by Leisure Press. Reprinted by permission.

Leisure Press books are available at special discounts for bulk purchase for sales promotions, premiums, fund-raising, or educational use. Special editions or book excerpts can also be created to specification. For details, contact the Special Sales Manager at Leisure Press.

Printed in the United States of America

10 9 8 7 6 5 4 3 2 1

Leisure Press
A Division of Human Kinetics Publishers, Inc.
Box 5076, Champaign, IL 61825-5076
1-800-747-4457

Canada Office:
Human Kinetics Publishers, Inc.
P.O. Box 2503, Windsor, ON N8Y 4S2
1-800-465-7301 (in Canada only)

Europe Office:
Human Kinetics Publishers (Europe) Ltd.
P.O. Box IW14
Leeds LS16 6TR
England
0532-781708

Contents

Series Preface

The Steps to Success Activity Series is a breakthrough in skill instruction through the development of complete learning progressions—the *steps to success*. These *steps* help individuals quickly perform basic skills successfully and prepare them to acquire more advanced skills readily. At each step, you are encouraged to learn at your own pace and to integrate your new skills into the total action of the activity.

The unique features of the Steps to Success Activity Series are the result of comprehensive development—analyzing existing activity books, incorporating the latest research from the sport sciences, and consulting with students, instructors, teacher educators, and administrators. This groundwork pointed up the need for three different types of books—for participants, instructors, and teacher educators—which we have created and together comprise the Steps to Success Activity Series.

This participant's book, *Advanced Golf: Steps to Success*, is a second-level golf text that follows the highly successful *Golf: Steps to Success*. That text guided the beginning golfer on a step-by-step process for learning the basic stroke fundamentals. Both books are self-paced, step-by-step guides that you can use as instructional tools to improve your game. The unique features of this participant's book include

- sequential illustrations that clearly show proper technique,
- helpful suggestions for detecting and correcting errors,
- excellent drill progressions with accompanying *Success Goals* for measuring performance, and
- checklists for rating technique.

Many of the activities in the Steps to Success Activity Series also have a comprehensive instructor's guide. *Teaching Golf: Steps to Success* accompanies the beginning-level text, but an instructor's guide has not been developed for this advanced-level text.

The series textbook, *Instructional Design for Teaching Physical Activities* (Vickers, 1990), explains the *steps to success* model, which is the basis for the Steps to Success Activity Series. Teacher educators can use the series textbook in their professional preparation classes to help future teachers and coaches learn how to design effective physical activity programs in school, recreation, or community teaching and coaching settings.

After identifying the need for various texts, we refined the *steps to success* instructional design model and developed prototypes. Once these prototypes were fine-tuned, we carefully selected authors for the activities who were not only thoroughly familiar with their sports but also had years of experience in teaching them. Each author had to be known as a gifted instructor who understands the teaching of sport so thoroughly that he or she could readily apply the *steps to success* model.

Next, all of the manuscripts were carefully developed to meet the guidelines of the *steps to success* model. Then our production team, along with outstanding artists, created a highly visual, user-friendly series of books.

The result: The Steps to Success Activity Series is the premier sports instructional series available today.

This series would not have been possible without the contributions of the following:

- Dr. Rainer Martens, Publisher
- Dr. Joan Vickers, instructional design expert
- The staff of Human Kinetics Publishers
- The *many* students, teachers, coaches, consultants, teacher educators, specialists, and administrators who shared their ideas—and dreams.

Judy Patterson Wright
Series Editor

Preface

This book is designed for experienced golfers who want to refine their skills and learn more about the game. You will learn advanced techniques related to swings, along with strategies for controlling attention and anxiety during competition. The many drills and self-evaluation techniques we present will help even the most advanced golfers reduce their handicap and enjoy the game more.

Advanced Golf: Steps to Success offers a step-by-step process for gaining the confidence and skill necessary to be a low-handicap golfer. A follow-up to the successful *Golf: Steps to Success*, it includes such advanced techniques as hitting draws and fades, options for sand play, advanced strategies for course management, off-green putting, and variations in pitch shots. Sections on playing in the wind and rain, mastering the mental aspects of golf, enjoying various playing formats (scrambles, best ball, nassaus, etc.), and calculating your handicap further enrich the content of the book.

We wrote *Advanced Golf* to help you make your practices fun and your play more efficient. Take it along to the practice tee as a reference for reviewing techniques and as a guide to better practice as you do the drills and record your scores. The activities are designed to motivate you and to help you become a self-learner who will enjoy golf for a lifetime.

We would like to acknowledge the contributions of those who have helped us bring this book into being. Cathy Vrdolyak and Diane Wakat provided both support and assistance in preparing the manuscript. Judy Patterson Wright, our developmental editor, provided excellent advice and managerial expertise as she coordinated the copyediting and illustrations.

We dedicate the book to our parents, Tony and Billie Bunker and Charles and Margaret Owens, who continually challenged us to be the best that we could be. We also thank the Jemsek family, owners of Cog Hill Golf Course in Lemont, Illinois, for the opportunity to continually test and refine our teaching philosophy. And our appreciation goes to colleagues who have influenced us—our values have been shaped by interactions with outstanding educators and golf professionals too numerous to individually name.

The Steps to Success Staircase

As an experienced golfer, you have built a foundation of golf skills and are ready to take the next steps to success. *Advanced Golf* builds on the fundamentals introduced in our beginners' book, *Golf: Steps to Success*, which is a good resource for any golfer to have on hand. Even the professionals go back to the fundamentals when their games go off.

This advanced book will lead you from perfecting fundamental strokes into the realm of challenge shots. Each of the 14 steps you will take is an easy transition from the one before. The first few steps of the staircase help you learn how to control ball curvature. As you progress farther, you will increase your options for approach shots and off-green putting and learn to putt with greater precision by reading greens more accurately. As you near the top of the staircase, you will learn how to use mental focus and visualization to hit more consistently and confidently, how to make better course management decisions, and how to adapt to various climates and conditions.

Now prepare to continue your journey to excellence. This text will lead you into a higher level of competitive golf. It will give your practice sessions more purpose and direction—as well as fun! Follow the same sequence each step (chapter) of the way:

1. Read the explanation of what is covered in the step, why the step is important, and how to execute or perform the step's focus, which may be a new skill, concept, tactic, or a combination.
2. Follow the numbered illustrations, which break down exactly how to position and move your body to perform each skill successfully. There are three phases in each skill breakdown: preparation (setup), execution (backswing and forwardswing), and follow-through.
3. Look over the common errors that may occur and the recommendations correcting them.
4. Practice the drills, which are specifically designed to help you achieve success at each step. Read the directions and the Success Goal for each drill. Practice accordingly and record your scores. Compare your scores with the Success Goal for the drill. You need to meet the Success Goal of each drill before moving on to practice the next one, because the drills are arranged in an easy-to-difficult progression.
5. After mastering each new skill, ask an expert, such as your teacher or golf pro, to evaluate your technique qualitatively according to the Keys to Success Checklist. Your evaluator may help you identify specific goals for your continued skill development.
6. Continue these procedures for each of the 14 Steps to Success. Then rate yourself and ask an expert to rate your total progress according to the Rating Your Progress directions.

Read the information in Appendix A, ''Clubs That Can Change Your Game,'' to determine if changing your club selection may improve your game. Appendix B contains a unique Shotkeeper Scorecard for recording your game play (and for use with some of the later drills).

Good luck on your step-by-step journey to increasing your golf skills, success, confidence, and fun. Climb at your own pace, and enjoy each step along the way.

Step 1 Swing Fundamentals

What do we really know about the golf swing? This much:

- It is designed to propel a small spherical object with varying configurations of dimples toward a 4-1/4-inch hole in the ground.
- It uses movement of the entire body to control a long object that serves as an extension of the arms.
- The flight of the ball is the result of how the club contacts the ball at impact.

Sound complex? Well, it is, if you get into deep biomechanical analysis. That's what makes the game so intriguing. But we'll be looking at it in simpler terms.

When you play golf, you are trying to predict and control ball flight, which is the combination of three factors: distance, direction, and trajectory. By developing consistent swing fundamentals and by understanding five laws derived from physics that govern ball flight, you open up options for creating a variety of shots to apply to situations on the course. In Step 1 we'll get you started on the road to this goal.

WHY IS IT IMPORTANT TO UNDERSTAND THE SWING?

The search for the perfect swing has motivated many of us to ask questions, identify our mistakes, and continue practicing. But golf professionals and teachers have learned that there is no single ''perfect'' swing. However, a consistent, effective swing is achievable, and it is the key to shooting lower scores. But what makes a swing effective?

Effective swinging involves controlling the three components of ball flight. Consider the ball flight results for these hypothetical golfers:

- Golfer A: Consistently hits a slice (a ball that curves excessively in the direction of the golfer's dominant hand); usually can predict the direction of the ball, but not the amount of curvature; has trouble both predicting and achieving distance and trajectory control.
- Golfer B: Inconsistent ball flight—may hit the ball a long way, but has no idea where it is going; sometimes hits a slice, other times a hook (a ball that curves excessively away from the direction of the golfer's dominant hand); never knows which direction the ball is going to travel; has a problem with inconsistent distance and trajectory control.
- Golfer C: Consistently hits a draw (a less-pronounced hook); has consistent distance, direction, and trajectory control.
- Golfer D: Hits long and consistently hits a fade (a less-pronounced slice); has consistent distance, direction, and trajectory control.

Which golfer do you think has the best chance for shooting the lowest scores, and why? If you select C or D, you're on the right track. Consistency allows for predictability.

Note that golfers C and D, though both hit consistently, have different ball flights. For golfers seeking greater distance, golfer C's ball flight, which creates a draw, is most desirable. For golfers who already hit the ball a long way— but often as a hook—a fade is usually the preferred shot because it gives greater direction control.

The fundamental concepts of golf technique, like any sport skill, derive from the science of physics. The Laws, Principles, and Preferences model created by Dr. Gary Wiren (1976) helps explain the golf swing in terms of physical *laws*, swing fundamentals (*principles*), and the options (*preferences*) you have for applying your knowledge of both on the course.

Consider a basic chip shot. When you chip, you gain distance control by removing wrist motion. This reduces the speed of the club (one of the factors in ball flight) as it contacts the ball. By the same token, if you eliminate the wrist cock in your full swing, the ball does not go as far. The wrist motion creates a levering system that is a source of clubhead speed.

So if you understand ball flight laws (e.g., speed determines distance) and swing fundamentals (e.g., how to control wrist cock), you can develop a more consistent and effective swing. You're able to become your own teacher and analyze your game (like why you always slice, or why your ball repeatedly lands short).

BALL FLIGHT LAWS

The five physical laws of ball flight are invariable, no matter who swings the club or where or how a club contacts the ball:

- Clubhead speed—The speed a club is traveling when it makes solid contact with a ball determines how far the ball will go.
- Clubhead path—A ball's starting direction is determined in part by the line along which the clubhead swings as it contacts the ball.
- Clubhead face—The direction of a ball is determined in part by the alignment of the clubhead face to the path of the swing.
- Angle of approach—Trajectory is determined by the angle of the golf club as it approaches the ball.
- Centeredness of club contact—How closely to the center of the clubhead face a ball is struck influences its distance and direction.

Whether you're John Daley (in 1991 the longest hitter on the men's PGA tour) or Cathy Smith (a senior women's club champion), your golf ball will move according to the ball flight laws. Let's look at each law in more detail.

Clubhead Speed

There is no substitute for swing speed. All other things being equal, a clubhead swung faster will always send the ball farther. Of course, there may be trade-offs in accuracy and control if you swing too fast and lose your balance—you must learn to control your body and the timing of your swing. Researchers have found that once you reach about 65 percent of your maximum speed, the accuracy of your swing actually increases. Most good golfers swing at 65 to 80 percent of maximum.

Clubhead Path

Imagine a wagon wheel on edge in front of you on the ground, with the edge aligned toward your target and the wheel tilted toward you about 45 degrees, forming an "inclined plane" (see Figure 1.1). At address, the ball is at the bottom of your imaginary wheel. The ideal swing follows a circular path—not perpendicular to the ground, as you might imagine, but on this wagon wheel incline. The swing moves along the wheel on the backswing, slightly inside the

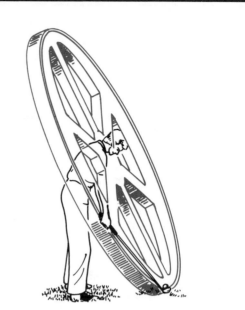

Figure 1.1 Wagon wheel forming an "inclined plane." The ideal swing follows a circular path on this incline.

wheel on the forwardswing, along the wheel just before and after impact, and slightly inside the wheel on the follow-through.

Keeping the wagon wheel image in mind, look at the possible ball flight patterns illustrated in Figure 1.2. A swing path that contacts the ball from the inside of the wheel yields a push (the ball lands to the dominant-hand side of the target line) and a path that contacts the ball from the outside of the wheel is a pull (the ball lands opposite to the dominant-hand side of the target line).

Clubhead Face

The face of the club can be square to the path, open, or closed (see Figure 1.3, a-c). The degree to which the clubface is open or closed at impact determines the amount of sidespin imparted to the ball. This spin causes the path of the ball to curve as the ball begins to slow down. Hooks and draws are produced by a closed clubface; slices and fades by an open clubface (review Figure 1.2).

Angle of Approach

Both the angle of the golf club as it approaches the ball (see Figure 1.4, a-d) and the loft of the club (the angle of the face away from vertical) determine the height of ball flight. The greater the loft, the higher and shorter the flight. Each

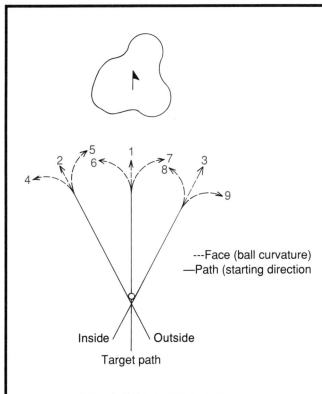

---Face (ball curvature)
—Path (starting direction

Inside / \ Outside

Target path

Nine possible ball flight patterns
(labeled for right handed golfers):
1. straight
2. pull
3. push
4. pull hook
5. pull slice
6. straight hook
7. straight slice
8. push hook
9. push slice

Figure 1.2 Ball flight patterns.

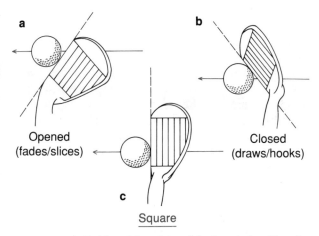

Opened
(fades/slices)

Closed
(draws/hooks)

c

Square

Figure 1.3 Clubhead face for a right-handed golfer. A square clubhead at contact produces little or no spin on the ball (c), an open face produces a slice/fade (a), and a closed clubface produces a hook/draw (b).

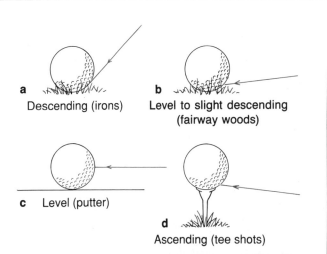

a Descending (irons)

b Level to slight descending (fairway woods)

c Level (putter)

d Ascending (tee shots)

Figure 1.4 Angle of approach for a right-handed golfer.

club can produce a range of trajectories, controlled by the loft of the club as it contacts the ball.

A ball struck above its centerline will have a low trajectory. The "worm-burner" that never gets airborne has usually been struck above the centerline. A ball struck below its centerline flies higher and makes best use of the club loft. Imagine the earth and its equator—each time you strike the ball, think about hitting below the equator, in South America or Australia or Africa.

Centeredness of Club Contact

A golf club is designed to strike near the center of its face. Just as a tennis racket has a "sweet spot," a golf club has a special point, called the "centroid," that produces maximum results in distance and direction control (See Figure 1.5).

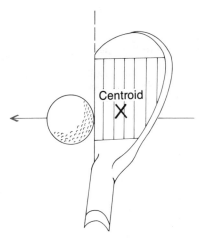

Centroid
X

Figure 1.5 Squareness of contact.

By striking the ball near the centroid of the club, you contact the ball more solidly and with better control. As the contact points move toward the heel or the toe of the club, distance and control errors are more likely.

PRESWING AND IN-SWING FUNDAMENTALS

The golf swing is a whole motion, with every part working in concert with all the others. Swing fundamentals, though, are divided into two components, those addressed before you swing and others of concern during your swing. Your execution of the fundamentals relates directly to your ball flight and to your ability to create an effective swing. For example, if you align your body too far right or left of your target, it will be difficult to get your clubhead to swing on path.

First we'll list the fundamentals, then we'll go on to describe them in more detail:

Preswing

- Grip
- Aim
- Setup

In-swing

- Plane of swing
- Width of arc
- Length of arc
- Target hand and wrist position
- Levers
- Timing
- Release
- Dynamic balance
- Swing center

Preswing Fundamentals

The preswing fundamentals involve getting your body and your club into position to produce an efficient swing. Consistent grip, aim, and setup build the foundation of a consistent swing motion.

Grip

How you grip your club influences how you interact with the ball—the club controls the ball, and your hands control the club. There are three grip variations: overlap, interlock, and 10-finger (see Figure 1.6, a-c). The overlap and interlock grips are generally preferred because they en-

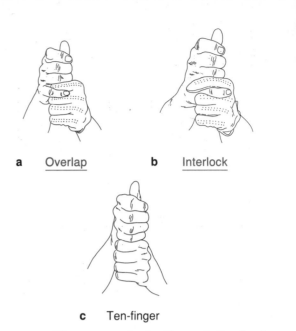

a Overlap **b** Interlock

c Ten-finger

Figure 1.6 Three types of grip. The underlined grips are preferred.

courage the hands to work together. Learn to place your hands on the club exactly the same way every time.

There are also choices to be made regarding the placement of the target and rear hands: top, neutral, or under. We recommend that both hands be positioned in a neutral grip. If the target hand is in a top position and the rear hand in an under position, the hands create excessive wrist movement; wrist motion is decreased too much if the hand placement is reversed. Either scenario creates a potential lack of consistency in distance and direction.

Aim

The alignment of your body and the clubface as you begin to swing is crucial to the resulting ball flight. When you stand at address in a neutral, or square, position, the clubface should be aligned square to the target (perpendicular to the line between ball and target). Your body (feet, hips, and shoulders) should be aligned parallel to the target line (see Figure 1.7). This alignment lets the club swing on the intended path for a longer time.

In this square position, the body can enhance the arm swing rather than restrict its motion in either direction. Remember, you want to establish a swing in which the arms and body work with, not against, each other. Alternatives to a square alignment of body and clubface (options toward open or closed) influence the path of the

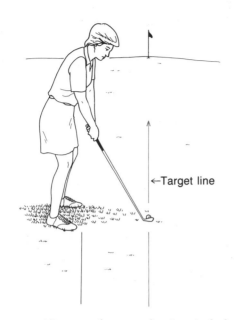

←Target line

Figure 1.7 Alignment for normal swings includes having the feet, hips, and shoulders parallel to the intended target line.

club relative to the target line and consequently the path of ball flight.

Setup

Your setup, a "ready position" that allows the body to easily swing the club, can influence your ball flight relative to each of the five laws. Setup includes posture, stance, weight distribution, and the placement of the ball relative to the body. The more consistent your setup, the more consistent your swing.

The position of your ball at address affects the angle of approach and the resulting trajectory. Ball placement is described relative to the tar-

get and the ball's position between the feet: back of center, center, or forward of center. Playing a ball forward in the stance, as in the driver setup, reduces the angle of approach if the swing center remains behind the ball at contact. This results in a higher trajectory. In contrast, playing a ball farther back (away from the target), as in the chip shot, increases the angle of approach, which results in a lower trajectory (review Figure 1.4, a-d) if the swing center remains in front of the ball.

Your weight distribution at address is another important aspect of setup. Keeping weight from your instep to the balls of your feet allows for ease of motion in the swing. You also want to keep weight evenly distributed between your feet.

In-Swing Fundamentals

The in-swing fundamentals are those components that take place during the swing motion.

Plane of Swing

The plane of your swing, an imaginary line that extends from the ball through and above your rear shoulder, is very important. Your ideal plane is determined by your posture at address. A golfer who stands far away from the ball will have a rather flat plane, whereas one who stands closer to the ball and more upright will have an upright plane. The level of plane can thus vary from flat to neutral (in-plane) to upright (see Figure 1.8, a-c).

At the top of the swing, if the target hand and arm are below the shoulder line the swing is flat. If the target hand and arm are above the shoulder with a space between the shoulder and arm

a Upright   **b** In-plane   **c** Flat

Figure 1.8 Plane of swing.

the swing is upright. In the neutral (in-plane) position, the target hand and arm are on the imaginary line that extends from the ball through and above the rear shoulder at address. The plane affects the clubpath at impact.

Width of Arc

Width and length are the aspects of the swing arc that primarily affect the distance the ball will travel. The width of the arc is the radius of the swing. Assume that your target arm is the radius of a circle. The longer the radius, the more potential speed the clubhead can develop. So, theoretically, the more extended your arm, the more speed (see Figure 1.9a) you have. But this does not mean to hold your arm stiff; it cannot get any longer than it already is. Simply maintain its length at both setup and ball contact. If you bend your arm, the width (radius) of the arc shortens and reduces the potential speed of the clubhead (see Figure 1.9b). *Note*: the underlined figures are preferred.

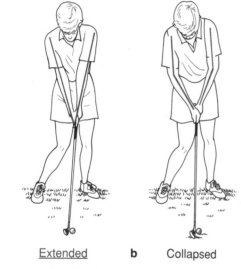

a   <u>Extended</u>   **b**   Collapsed

Figure 1.9 Width of arc.

Length of Arc

The length of the swing arc (your backswing) determines the potential speed in your forwardswing. For a short putt, you take a short backswing. For longer shots you take longer backswings, so that the forwardswing has more time and space to develop speed.

The speed in your forwardswing transfers directly into force imparted to the ball and therefore to the distance the ball travels. The greater the backswing, the greater the potential speed and potential distance. For most golfers the op-

timal swing length places the club shaft parallel to the ground at the top of the backswing (see Figure 1.10, a-c).

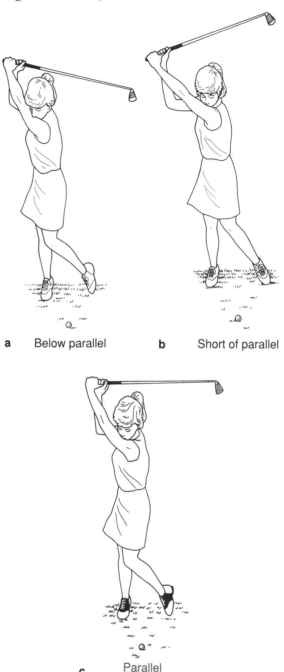

a   Below parallel   **b**   Short of parallel

c   <u>Parallel</u>

Figure 1.10 Length of arc.

Target Hand and Wrist Position

The relationship between your target hand and arm and the club at the top of your swing is very important. By simply changing the wrist position of your target hand from extended to cocked, you can dramatically affect the position of the clubface at the top of the backswing and consequently your ability to return the clubface to its original starting position at ball contact. To increase your consistency and efficiency, your hand should be square, rather than cupped or flexed, at the top of the swing (see Figure 1.11, a-c).

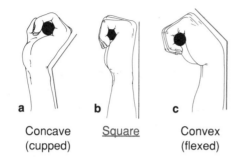

a	b	c
Concave (cupped)	<u>Square</u>	Convex (flexed)

Figure 1.11 Position of hands at top for a right-handed golfer.

Your target and rear hand positions at the top of the backswing are predetermined by maintaining your grip position at address. You can see and feel this position by taking your address position, and cock your wrists upward. This allows the club to cock in plane with your arms.

Levers

The target arm and club act as one long lever. If you allow your wrist to cock in plane with your forearm, without flexing it forward or backward, you add a second lever and approximately double your potential force (see Figure 1.12, b). A third lever can be created by bending your elbow. However, this adds potential swing error because it is more difficult to get the three levers timed at impact.

Timing

The sequence of movements in the golf swing must be timed carefully for efficiency and ease of motion. The backswing timing builds from the initial take-away of the clubhead from the ball, through the arms, shoulders, hips, and legs and then returns in the reverse order. The motion is like a coil tightening and then unwinding. You can think of this motion as having three parts: hands and arms, then shoulders, and finally hips and legs, winding up in that order. Then the forwardswing starts, first with the legs and hips, then the shoulders, and lastly the arms and hands (1-2-3, 3-2-1).

Release

At the moment of ball contact, your hands and arms should have returned to their original position. The clubface attains its maximum speed

a One-lever swing	b <u>Two-lever swing</u>	c Three-lever swing

Figure 1.12 Levers in the swing.

and square alignment as you "release" your hands and forearms, creating a timed release. This is not a natural movement, but it is one you can learn.

The hands act like an extra lever in the total action of the swing. At address, your thumb points down at the ball. As your hands and arms swing the club away from the ball, your arms rotate and the thumbs point up (like a hitch-hiker's). As your arms return during the forwardswing, your thumbs point at the ball again, then up again as the follow-through begins.

Releasing early and releasing late are common errors that reduce the potential clubhead speed and cause direction problems. In an early release, often referred to as "casting" or "throwing the club," the hands begin to uncock too soon and throw the timing out of sequence. The arm swing slows down and the hands work almost independently of the overall motion of the swing. In a late release, the wrist cock is retained beyond the ball. This is often caused by a very tight grip pressure, resulting in less speed and a tendency to push the ball. Compare the releases shown in Figure 1.13, a-c.

Dynamic Balance

An effective golf swing requires that you maintain overall body balance as you swing your arms and rotate your trunk (see Figure 1.14, a-

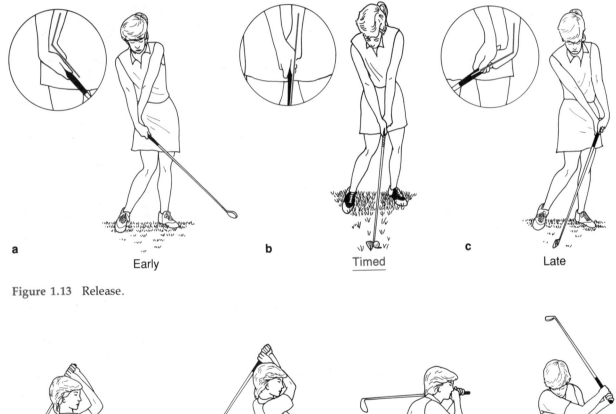

a Early   b Timed   c Late

Figure 1.13 Release.

a Falls back   b Controlled   c Falls forward   d Stationary

Figure 1.14 Dynamic balance.

d). The objective is to transfer to the ball all of the energy acquired in the backswing. You start with your body aligned with the ball, through a pivoting motion, then you rotate your weight away from the target and then back through the ball to a follow-through toward the target. If your body does not pass back through your starting position, you will lose power, alter the arc of the swing and point of impact, and lose distance and accuracy. The key is to practice swinging so that, in each forwardswing, the bottom of the arc and the rest of your body are at the same point each time.

Swing Center

The golf swing can be imagined as a wagon wheel inclined along the plane of swing (review Figure 1.1). The center of the wheel lies somewhere near the center of your sternum. This "swing center" is an imaginary point around which the arc is made.

Most good golfers shift their swing centers slightly away from the ball as the body rotates around the spine on the backswing. The key is on the forwardswing to get your swing center back over the ball, into its original starting position, at contact. The traditional teaching cue "Keep your head down" was designed to emphasize the importance of maintaining a constant swing center. However, a concentrated effort to keep the head down results in reducing the effective swing motion. Use the thought of maintaining your swing center as a cue, instead, to remind you to return to your original position over the ball, so that the arc of your swing does not change.

Your golf swing is an expression of your understanding of the laws of ball flight and your application of the swing fundamentals. Knowing how both work should help you diagnose any problems in your swing and work toward correcting them.

SWING FUNDAMENTALS AND OPTIONS CHECKLIST

The Keys to Success Checklist (Figure 1.15) summarizes the various swing fundamentals and their components that we have discussed in Step 1. For each element, we have asterisked the option preferred by most good golfers; a swing that combines these asterisked options will create a ball flight that starts on target with a slight draw.

You can either check yourself in a mirror or use an observer (who is familiar with the options). For effective analysis, your observer needs to be positioned either directly in front of you (looking face on) or behind you and to the side (looking down the target line). These positions are designated *front view* and *down-the-line view* in the checklist. If you find you have a mixture of characteristics, some with asterisks and others without, you need to make some adjustments to be more consistent with the suggested fundamentals and options.

Figure 1.15 Keys to Success Checklist: Swing Fundamentals and Options
(*indicates preferred)

Preparation (Preswing) Phase

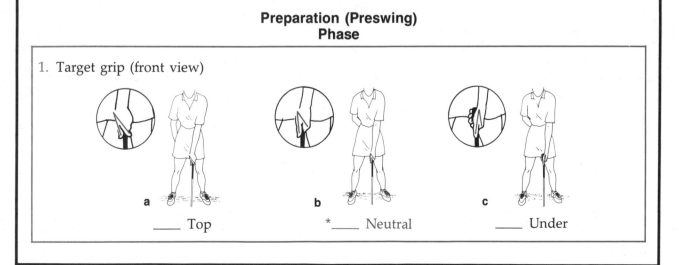

1. Target grip (front view)

a ____ Top   *____ Neutral b   c ____ Under

2. Rear grip (front view)

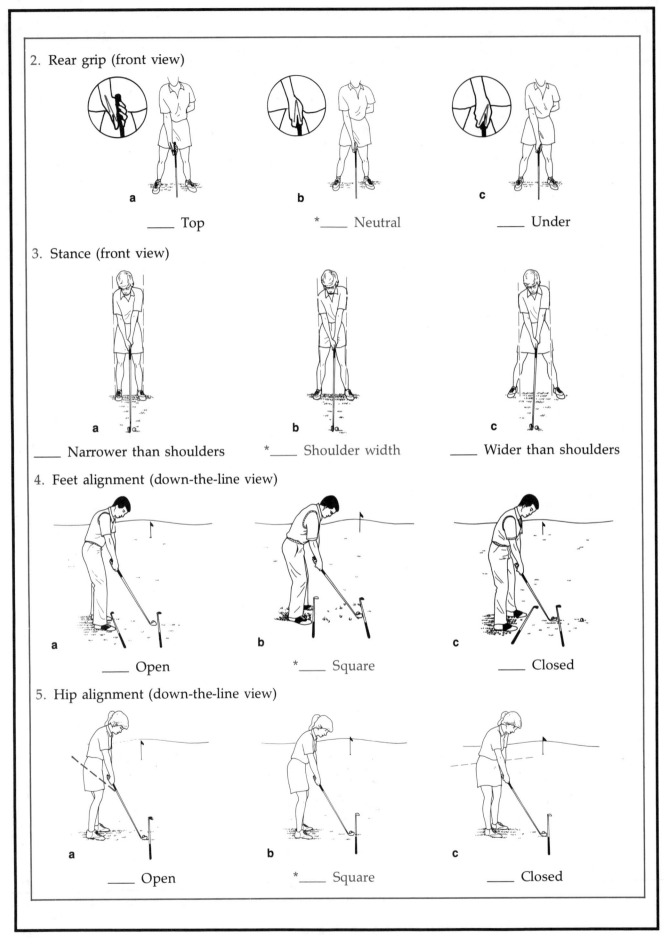

a

____ Top

b

*____ Neutral

c

____ Under

3. Stance (front view)

a

____ Narrower than shoulders

b

*____ Shoulder width

c

____ Wider than shoulders

4. Feet alignment (down-the-line view)

a

____ Open

b

*____ Square

c

____ Closed

5. Hip alignment (down-the-line view)

a

____ Open

b

*____ Square

c

____ Closed

6. Shoulder alignment (down-the-line view)

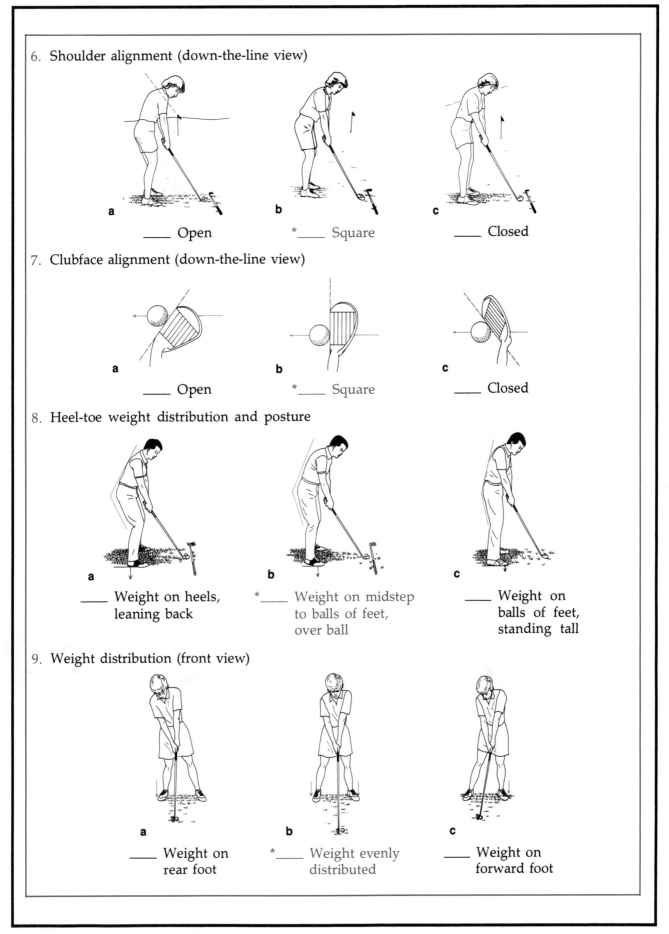

a

____ Open

b

*____ Square

c

____ Closed

7. Clubface alignment (down-the-line view)

a

____ Open

b

*____ Square

c

____ Closed

8. Heel-toe weight distribution and posture

a

____ Weight on heels,
leaning back

b

*____ Weight on midstep
to balls of feet,
over ball

c

____ Weight on
balls of feet,
standing tall

9. Weight distribution (front view)

a

____ Weight on
rear foot

b

*____ Weight evenly
distributed

c

____ Weight on
forward foot

10. Address swing center (front view)

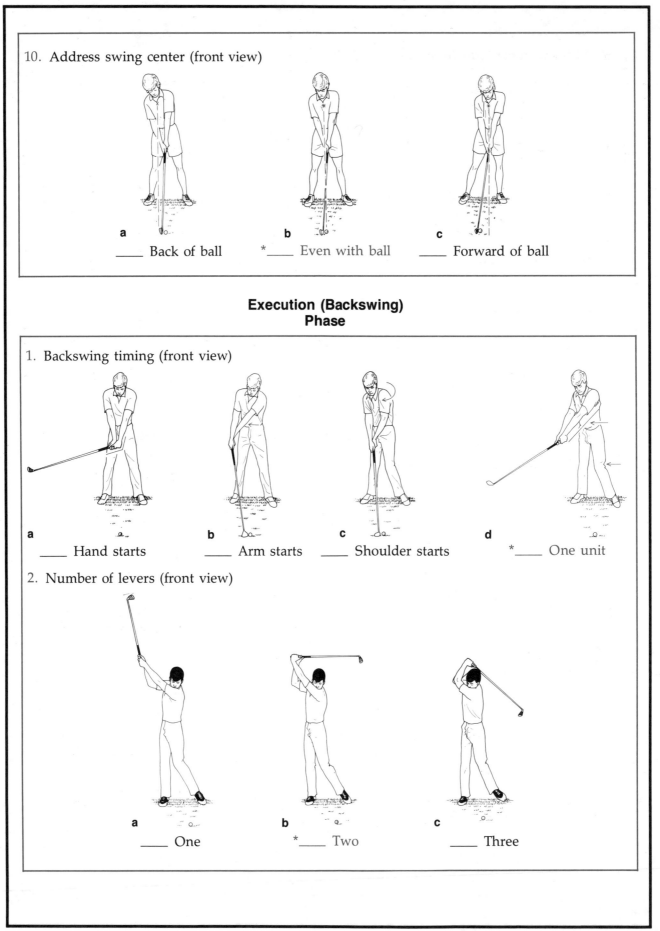

_____ Back of ball   *_____ Even with ball   _____ Forward of ball

Execution (Backswing) Phase

1. Backswing timing (front view)

_____ Hand starts   _____ Arm starts   _____ Shoulder starts   *_____ One unit

2. Number of levers (front view)

_____ One   *_____ Two   _____ Three

3. Length of arc (front view)

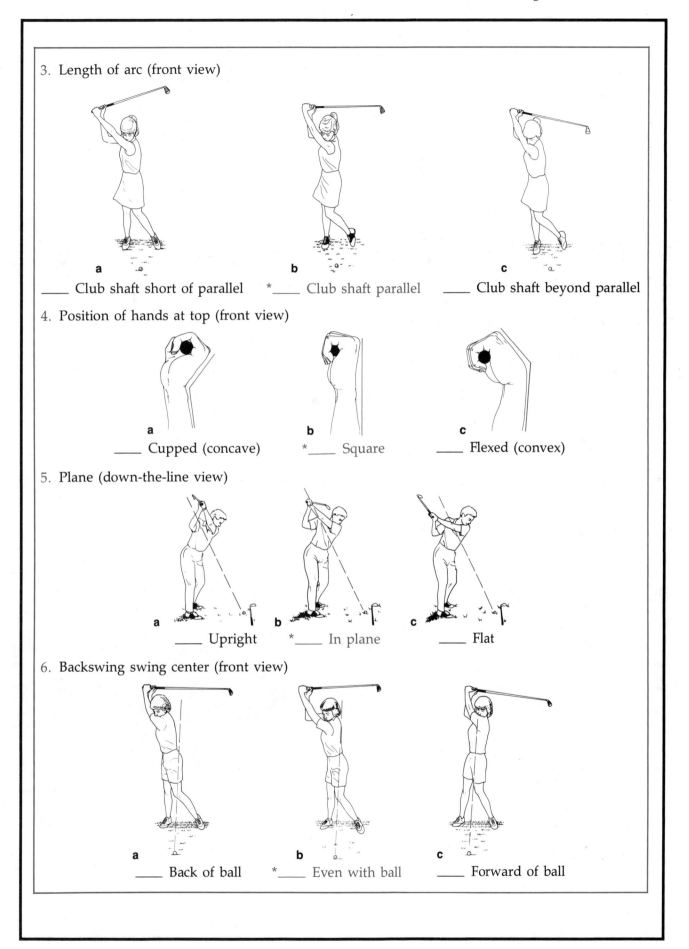

                         a   b   c

____ Club shaft short of parallel   *____ Club shaft parallel   ____ Club shaft beyond parallel

4. Position of hands at top (front view)

                         a   b   c

____ Cupped (concave)   *____ Square   ____ Flexed (convex)

5. Plane (down-the-line view)

                         a   b   c

____ Upright   *____ In plane   ____ Flat

6. Backswing swing center (front view)

                         a   b   c

____ Back of ball   *____ Even with ball   ____ Forward of ball

Execution (Forwardswing)
Phase

1. Forwardswing timing (front view)

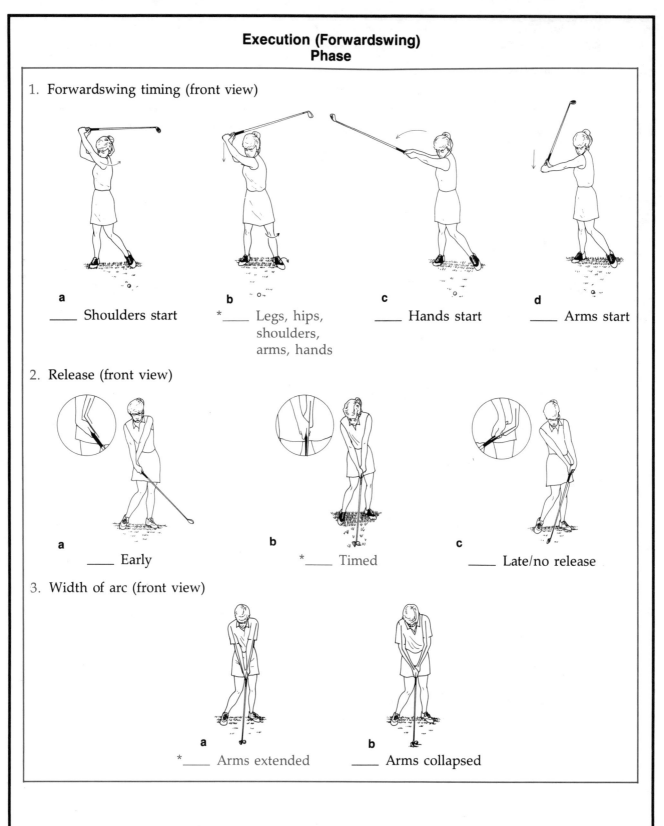

a
____ Shoulders start

b
*____ Legs, hips, shoulders, arms, hands

c
____ Hands start

d
____ Arms start

2. Release (front view)

a
____ Early

b
*____ Timed

c
____ Late/no release

3. Width of arc (front view)

a
*____ Arms extended

b
____ Arms collapsed

**Follow-Through
Phase**

1. Balance (front view)

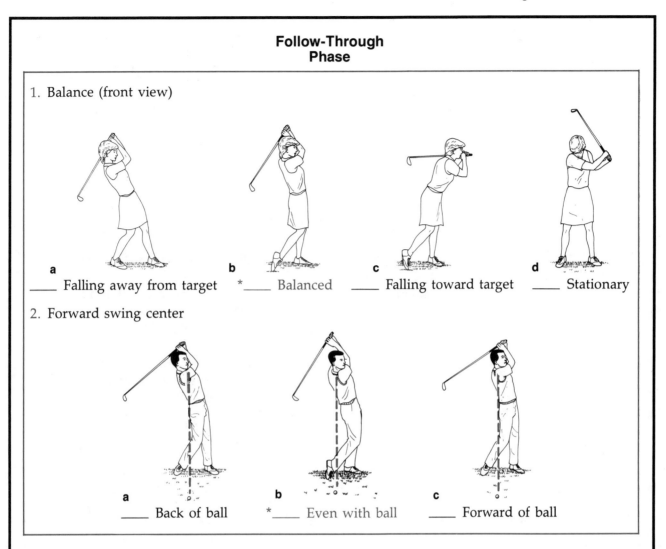

_____ Falling away from target   *_____ Balanced   _____ Falling toward target   _____ Stationary

a   b   c   d

2. Forward swing center

a   b   c

_____ Back of ball   *_____ Even with ball   _____ Forward of ball

In the rest of the book, you'll learn to apply your understanding of the laws and the swing fundamentals. By making alterations in the fundamentals for the full swing, you can create different ball flights for a variety of optional shots. For example, in executing a chip shot, a low ball flight is desired, using less swing speed to control the distance. Trajectory is controlled by the different ball positions in the stance. A comparison of the fundamentals needed to execute both the full swing and the chip shot follows:

Fundamentals	Full swing	Chip shot
Preswing		
a. Hip alignment	Square	Open
b. Feet alignment	Square	Open
c. Ball position	Forward	Back
d. Weight distribution	Even	Weight on target foot
e. Swing center	Even	Forward
In-swing		
a. Levers	2	1
b. Length of arc	Parallel	Short

Through practice, you will begin to feel in complete control of your game. Take the time to review Step 1 often. This is your foundation for improvement.

Detecting Errors in the Swing Fundamentals

Understanding the ball flight laws and the swing fundamentals will help you in the complete development of your game. By understanding basic concepts, you will not only better understand any instruction, but also you will ultimately become your own best teacher.

ERROR    **CORRECTION**

ERROR	CORRECTION
1. Ball travels straight but always lands left or right of target.	1. Check for path error—alignment is usually a major cause.
2. Ball starts out straight but then curves away from target.	2. Check clubface. Open and closed faces produce spin, causing the ball to hook or slice. Ineffective grips and lack of release are common causes.
3. The ball doesn't get airborne.	3. Angle of approach affects trajectory. Check your posture to be sure you are maintaining your swing center on your forwardswing. Your target arm should be extended, not bent, at impact.
4. Ball flight is too short.	4. Lack of distance is often caused by slow clubhead speed. Check for problems with timing or length of arc. Practice swinging with a faster swing speed.
5. Ball reacts sharply right or left.	5. Check for square contact, which is required for balls to travel straight ahead.
6. Balance is lost during follow-through of a drive, and an extra step is needed to regain balance.	6. Check that swing speed is not excessive and that weight is shifting through the swing motion, from address to rear side to target side.

Drills for Swing Fundamentals

1. Grip Drill

It is important to understand how changing your grip affects the resulting ball flight. Hit 9 balls, 3 with a neutral grip, 3 with a three-knuckle grip (rear hand on top of club), and 3 with the rear hand turned under the club and only one knuckle showing. Take a different grip for each swing. Practice this drill to develop clubface control and speed.

Success Goal = Hit 9 balls, using a different grip on each shot to observe the effects, and record the results

Your Score = Record grip changes and resultant ball flight changes

Grip position	Ball flight results
1. Neutral	_____
2. 3-knuckle	_____
3. 1-knuckle	_____
4. 3-knuckle	_____
5. Neutral	_____
6. 3-knuckle	_____
7. 1-knuckle	_____
8. Neutral	_____
9. 1-knuckle	_____

2. Aim and Setup Drill

As you begin your practice session, use two clubs placed parallel on the ground to help you get aligned. It is easy to get misaligned and then unknowingly build compensations into your swing.

Align one club parallel to the target line and slightly in front of it. Take your address position, then place the second club just in front of your feet, parallel to the target line.

Practice your alignment first without hitting balls; then hit balls using the clubs as a target reference, and finally practice without the alignment clubs.

Success Goal =

    a. Practice your alignment 5 times without hitting balls

    b. Hit 10 balls, setting the alignment clubs at a different target each time

    c. Hit 10 balls at different targets without using the alignment clubs

Your Score =

    a. (#) ____ times alignment practiced without hitting balls

    b. (#) ____ balls hit with clubs realigned between shots

    c. (#) ____ balls hit without alignment clubs

3. Extremes Drill

It is important to be able to produce extreme errors so you can understand how they occur and how to correct them. Try producing pushes and pulls versus slices and hooks. Use your knowledge of the laws of clubhead path and clubface to generate the desired paths and curvature.

Success Goal = Hit 15 balls: 3 pushes, 3 pulls, 3 slices, 3 hooks, and 3 shots down the middle (in random order)

Your Score = Indicate which shot you are attempting, the outcome, and whether the two matched

	Shot attempted	Outcome	Matched intent? Yes	Matched intent? No
Example	*Hook*	*Pull*		✓
Ball 1				
Ball 2				
Ball 3				
Ball 4				
Ball 5				
Ball 6				
Ball 7				
Ball 8				
Ball 9				
Ball 10				
Ball 11				
Ball 12				
Ball 13				
Ball 14				
Ball 15				
		TOTAL		

4. Bogey Golf

With a partner, play a game of "Bogey." Golfers alternate in specifying what shot is to be executed. Both players attempt the shot; anyone who errs earns a letter toward the word *bogey*. When either player completes the word, the game is over.

Success Goal = Hit every shot as specified

Your Score = _____ letters earned toward "bogey"

5. Baseball Path Drill

This is a fun way to practice your ball flight direction. The objective is to successfully hit balls where you want them to go; we'll explain the drill using a sample scenario.

   You start the round with 6 balls, which you assign in pairs to three piles: left field, center field, and right field.

      O O   O O   O O

    Left   Center   Right

Decide what shot you're going to use to hit a ball in a certain direction—let's say you decide to head for left field. Take a ball from the left field pair, then, and make the shot. Be sure always to align to your center field target, regardless of what direction you want to hit.

      O   O O   O O

    L   C   R

If your shot goes where you planned, great—choose another shot and repeat the task, using a ball from the direction you name. This time you decide on right field, leaving four balls in the piles.

This time you miss the mark—instead of hitting to right field, you send the ball to center. So you must lose a ball from center field (the direction you hit by mistake) and move it to right field (the direction you said you'd hit):

Again you decide to try for right field, but again you hit to center field. So you lose the remaining center field ball to the right field pile, leaving no balls in center field.

If you mis-hit to center field again, you lose the element of choice—simply move on to the remaining balls. Your goal is to hit all 6 balls to the intended locations, without forfeiting any to other piles.

Success Goal = Hit 6 consecutive balls to intended locations

Your Score = (#) _____ balls hit to intended locations

6. Angle of Approach Drill

Try varying your angle of approach in hitting balls. With a long (3) iron, use a steep angle of approach and make the ball look like it has been hit by a 9-iron. Practice changing the angle of approach and observe the difference in ball flight trajectories.

Success Goal = Use a 3-iron to hit four different angles of approach. (Imagine you are hitting under tree limbs of varying heights.) Note the difference in the ball's trajectory the steeper the angle of approach

Your Score = (#) _____ different trajectories produced with the same club

7. Distance Manipulation Drill

Create an imaginary target, about 20 feet in diameter and about 80 yards away. Practice getting a ball into the circle using four different clubs, such as a 9-iron, an 8-iron, a pitching wedge, and a 5-iron. Experiment with the technique necessary to produce an 80-yard swing each time, such as club speed, squareness of contact, angle of approach, and squareness of clubface alignment.

Success Goal = With 4 different clubs, hit balls to a target 80 yards away. Hit 3 balls with each club. Adjust your swing to produce an 80-yard shot with each club

Your Score = (#) _____ out of 12 shots hit into the target

Step 2 **Cont**

As a beginning golfer you had two major objectives. The first was to develop a consistent swing motion (which tends to create more consistent ball flight) in each of the various shots, such as the full swing, pitch, and chip. The second objective was to become comfortable playing on a course and to get familiar with the rules and etiquette of play.

As your skill improved and you became more relaxed, you probably noticed greater consistency in your ball flight. Playing on the course probably also required some creative shot-making that you may have felt unprepared for. Hitting from behind trees or under bushes is not difficult once you feel comfortable with your swing. Steps 2 through 8 focus on learning how to handle various situations that require altering your normal ball flight.

This step introduces you to controlling trajectory and creating ball flights higher and lower than normal. You also learn to control curvature and to produce intentional hooks and slices.

WHY IS CONTROLLING BALL FLIGHT IMPORTANT?

No one hits the ball in the fairway on every tee shot. As you advance in golf, you need a variety of more sophisticated shots to choose from. For example, what are your options if your ball lands behind a tree? If your ball is in a playable lie, you may have as many as four choices for your shot: sideways, under, over, or around the tree.

To go sideways, you can use your chip shot technique and get the ball back into play (though the ball might not be advanced toward your target). Hitting under, over, or around requires altering your normal ball flight. Learning to hit shots higher and lower and curving to the right and left can save you potentially three or more shots a round.

HOW TO EXECUTE BALL FLIGHT CONTROL

Controlling ball flight is not difficult; you use your normal full swing motion with only slight variations in your setup. The subtle changes required will add great variety and control to your game.

Trajec
Shots

The ball's of approac the amount the ball.

Imagine the b The north pole, represent the top, cen of the ball, respectively. To get the ball airborne, you must contact it below the equator. Your desired contact on the ball is the bottom or south pole. A ball that is contacted at or above the equator will have a lower flight than normal, if it gets airborne at all. You have probably experienced these "topped" or "thin" shots.

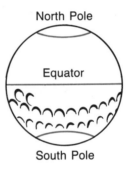

Figure 2.1 Ball as earth.

To control trajectory for higher and lower shots, you must change the normal loft of your clubface at impact. This can be accomplished with one basic change in ball position in your regular setup. You add loft to the clubface for a high shot by moving the ball forward of center and subtract it for a low shot by moving the ball back of center.

The same concept applies to both irons and woods, but the irons can tolerate a back-of-center position, while the woods can tolerate a more forward ball position.

Try this to visualize altering your ball position: Place eight balls in a row (see Figure 2.2). Ball 4 is the center of your stance. Balls 5 through 8 are on the target side, and balls 1 through 3 on the rear side. Ball 8 would be placed off the

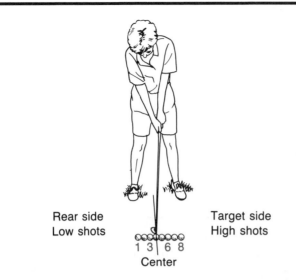

Rear side
Low shots

Target side
High shots

1 3 | 6 8
Center

Figure 2.2 Ball positions used to change trajectory. The center position is at Ball 4. For higher trajectories, place balls at positions 6 through 8. For low shots, use positions 1 through 3.

target toe, and Ball 1 off the rear heel. These are the extreme ball positions for a high shot (Ball 8) and a low shot (Ball 1).

If your normal ball position is 5 for an iron, your iron shots will vary for a high shot between Balls 6 and 7 and a low shot between Balls 4 and 1. The woods have less ball variation; high shots would be Ball 8 and possibly 7, depending on your normal position. Low shots should not be placed farther back than Ball 5 or 6. Through practice swings you can determine your normal ball position (where the club consistently contacts the ground). Note the ball position number. Then you can determine extremes for woods and irons.

The Keys to Success for trajectory control are presented in Figure 2.3 (the numbered ball positions refer to Figure 2.2). The ball position guidelines will help you develop greater consistency in trajectory control.

Figure 2.3 Keys to Success: Trajectory Control: High and Low Shots

(*indicates variation from normal swing)

Preparation Phase

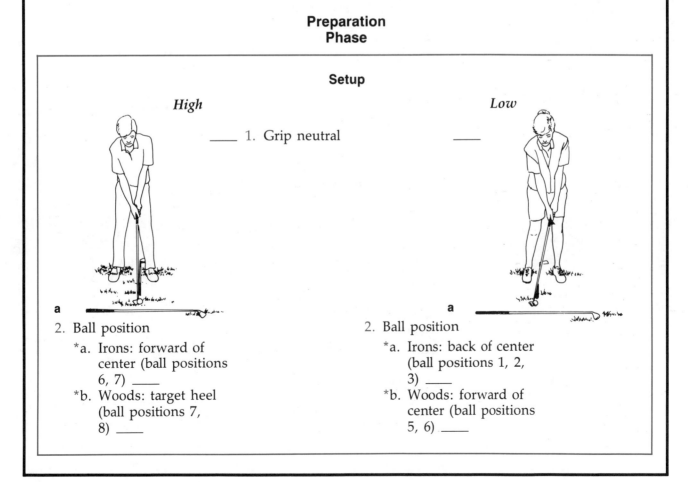

Setup

High

_____ 1. Grip neutral _____

Low

a   a

2. Ball position
   *a. Irons: forward of center (ball positions 6, 7) _____
   *b. Woods: target heel (ball positions 7, 8) _____

2. Ball position
   *a. Irons: back of center (ball positions 1, 2, 3) _____
   *b. Woods: forward of center (ball positions 5, 6) _____

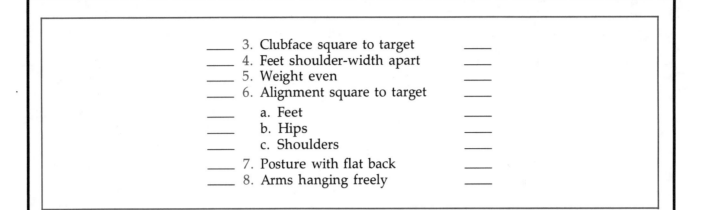

_____ 3. Clubface square to target _____
_____ 4. Feet shoulder-width apart _____
_____ 5. Weight even _____
_____ 6. Alignment square to target _____
_____   a. Feet _____
_____   b. Hips _____
_____   c. Shoulders _____
_____ 7. Posture with flat back _____
_____ 8. Arms hanging freely _____

Execution Phase

Backswing

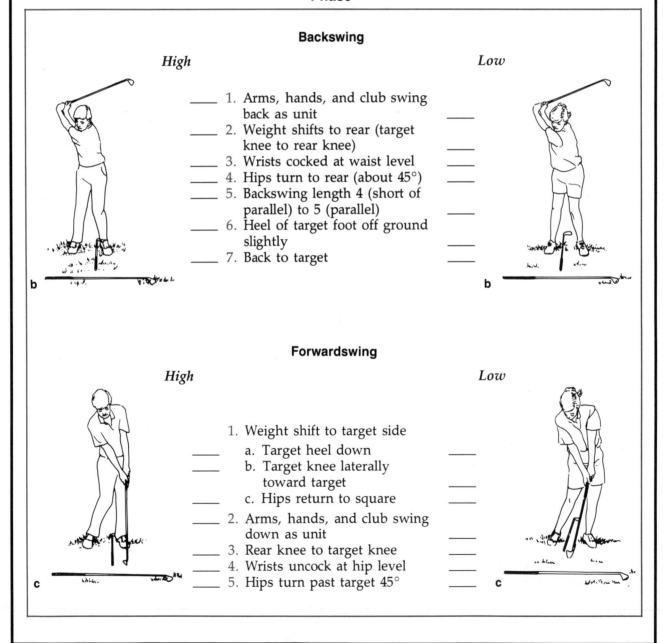

High   *Low*

_____ 1. Arms, hands, and club swing back as unit _____
_____ 2. Weight shifts to rear (target knee to rear knee) _____
_____ 3. Wrists cocked at waist level _____
_____ 4. Hips turn to rear (about 45°) _____
_____ 5. Backswing length 4 (short of parallel) to 5 (parallel) _____
_____ 6. Heel of target foot off ground slightly _____
_____ 7. Back to target _____

b   b

Forwardswing

High   *Low*

    1. Weight shift to target side
_____   a. Target heel down _____
_____   b. Target knee laterally toward target _____
_____   c. Hips return to square _____
_____ 2. Arms, hands, and club swing down as unit _____
_____ 3. Rear knee to target knee _____
_____ 4. Wrists uncock at hip level _____
_____ 5. Hips turn past target 45° _____

c   c

Follow-Through Phase

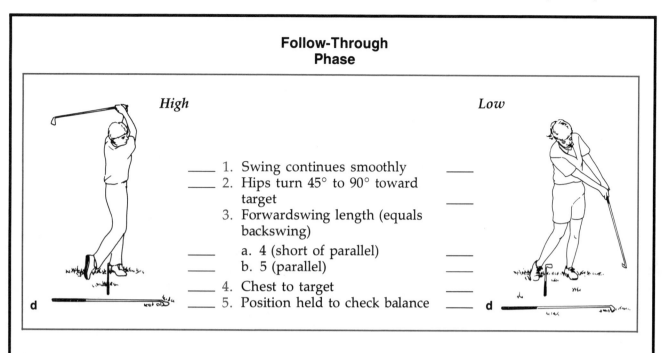

High   *Low*

_____ 1. Swing continues smoothly _____
_____ 2. Hips turn 45° to 90° toward target _____
3. Forwardswing length (equals backswing)
_____   a. 4 (short of parallel) _____
_____   b. 5 (parallel) _____
_____ 4. Chest to target _____
_____ 5. Position held to check balance _____

Curvature Control: Hooks and Slices

In Step 1 you learned that clubface position at impact, relative to your target direction, influences the curvature of ball flight (see Figure 1.2). The degree of curvature can vary from slight to severe, depending on how open or closed the clubface is at impact. An open clubface creates a fade (slight curvature) to a slice (excessive curvature). A closed clubface creates a draw (slight curvature) to a hook (excessive curvature).

There are several ways to control ball flight curvature: modifying your grip, changing grip pressure, and altering body alignment with clubface alignment. In this step we'll teach you how to control ball flight curvature and still use your regular full swing motion.

Grip Modification

The greatest influence on the clubface at impact is your grip: the *position* of your hands on the club and the amount of *pressure* in your hands as you contact the ball. The three grip positions are presented in Figure 2.4, a-c. You may have seen them referred to as strong, neutral, and weak, or hook, neutral, and slice. In the strong position (Figure 2.4a), with 3 to 4 knuckles of the target hand showing, your hands can be more active in the swing. The strong grip position helps create a closed clubface at impact and a draw-to-hook curvature. In the weak position (Figure 2.4c), only 1 to 1-1/2 knuckles are visible

on the target hand. This position tends to reduce hand action and create a more open clubface at impact and a fade-to-slice curvature. The neutral position (Figure 2.4b) has 2 to 2-1/2 knuckles showing on the target hand. The neutral position, which blends the strong and weak grips, is recommended by most golf teachers.

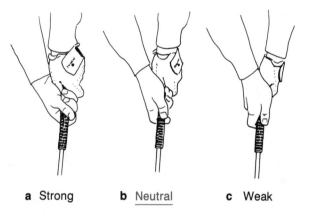

a Strong   **b** Neutral   **c** Weak

Figure 2.4 Grip positions influence ball curvature.

Grip pressure is the level of tension in your hands at impact. The degree of pressure affects the amount of hand action and corresponding clubface control. Light grip pressure encourages hand action and a draw-to-hook curvature, while tight pressure restricts hand action and tends to create a fade-to-slice curvature. Extremes in pressure tend to influence wide variations in ball flight curvature; you will need to find your own optimal pressure.

Alignment and Clubface Modification

Imagine yourself on the course; you're behind a tree and need to go around it toward your target (see Figure 2.5, a and b). This requires alignment and clubface modifications in your setup. The modified setup will feel awkward initially, but with practice you will be able to adjust. Note the differing ball curvatures; in Figure 2.5a the ball starts toward the fairway, then hooks toward the target; in Figure 2.5b it slices toward the target.

To accomplish the hook, align your clubface toward the ultimate target (through the tree), but align your stance and body toward an intermediate target, which is the direction you want the ball to start moving (around the tree). Then make your regular swing. The position of the clubface, open or closed to your intermediate target, creates the desired curvature, while your stance and swing motion control the path or starting direction of the ball.

To hit a slice around the tree, use the same principles. Align your clubhead square to your final target and your body with your intermediate target (see Figure 2.5b).

Figure 2.5 Keys to Success:
Clubface Control: Intentional Hooks and Slices
(*indicates variation from normal swing)

**Preparation
Phase**

Setup

Draw/Hook   *Fade/Slice*

*1. Grip strong ___   *1. Grip weak ___

___ 2. Feet shoulder-width apart   ___
___ 3. Weight even   ___
4. Alignment square to inter-
mediate target (direction the
ball starts in)
___   a. Feet   ___
___   b. Hips   ___
___   c. Shoulders   ___
___ 5. Posture with back flat   ___
___ 6. Arms hanging freely   ___
7. Ball position
___   a. Irons: near center   ___
___   b. Woods: target side of
center
*___ 8. Clubface square to final target *___

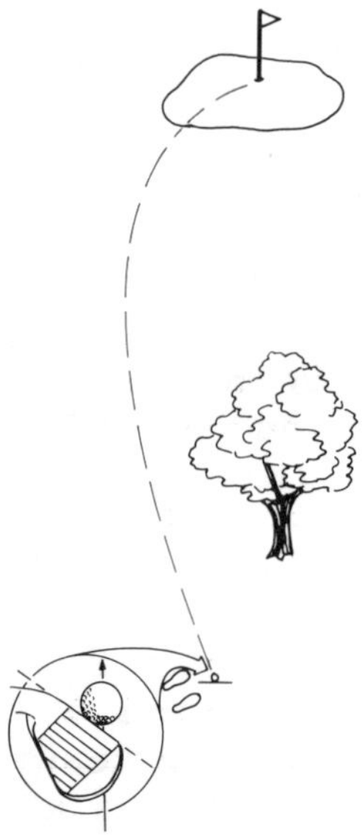

a   b

Execution
Phase

Backswing

Draw/Hook   *Fade/Slice*

____ 1. Arms, hands, and club
        swing back as unit   ____
____ 2. Weight shifts to rear (tar-
        get knee to rear knee)   ____
____ 3. Wrists cocked at waist
        level   ____
____ 4. Hips turn to rear (about
        45°)   ____
     5. Backswing length (based
        on distance to target):
____   a. 4 (short of parallel)   ____
____   b. 5 (parallel)   ____
____ 6. Heel of target foot off
        ground slightly   ____
____ 7. Back to target   ____

Forwardswing

Draw/Hook   *Fade/Slice*

     1. Weight shift to target side
____   a. Target heel down   ____
____   b. Target knee laterally
           toward target   ____
____   c. Hips return to square   ____
____ 2. Arms, hands, and club
        swing down as unit   ____
____ 3. Rear knee to target knee   ____
____ 4. Wrists uncock at hip level   ____
____ 5. Hips return through setup
        position (to 45°)   ____

**Follow-Through
Phase**

	Draw/Hook		*Fade/Slice*
____	1. Swing continues smoothly		____
____	2. Hips face target		____
	3. Forwardswing length (equals backswing):		
____	a. 4 (short of parallel)		____
____	b. 5 (parallel)		____
____	4. Chest to target		____
____	5. Position held to check balance		____

Detecting Trajectory and Curvature Errors

Review the following points as you begin to observe trajectory and curvature errors. Trajectory is influenced by ball position and the point of clubface-ball contact. Curvature is influenced by grip position, grip pressure, and setup. An open clubface at impact creates a fade/slice curvature, and a closed clubface at impact creates a draw/hook curvature.

ERROR   **CORRECTION**

1. With a 6-iron, ball flight is straight but low when you're trying to hit a high shot.	1. Contact ball below the center. Make practice swings clipping the grass. Be sure ball position is not too far forward for good contact with an iron.
2. In attempting a draw, you slice the ball.	2. Check your grip and grip pressure. Hit a draw with a neutral grip and medium-to-light pressure.
3. In trying to hit around a tree, you hit the tree instead.	3. Check your alignment. Your body should be parallel to your intermediate target and the clubface aligned toward your final target (see Figure 2.5).
4. You hit a low shot under the trees perfectly except for just catching the lower branch.	4. This may be a club selection error. It is better to take a club with less loft (lower number) than one you think will just make it under the limb.

Controlling Ball Flight Drills

1. High-Low Drill

The trajectory of a golf ball is affected by the clubhead's angle of approach at contact. Using a 7-iron, make your shots travel higher or lower by varying the ball position in your stance, thus adjusting the angle of approach.
Variation: Repeat this drill with your fairway woods.

Success Goal = Hit 12 balls, varying trajectory from low to normal to high

    a. 3 balls hit at a low trajectory (ball back of center)

    b. 3 balls hit at a normal trajectory (your normal ball position, or ball center to just forward of center)

    c. 3 balls hit at a high trajectory (ball forward of normal position)

    d. 1 ball hit at a low trajectory

    e. 1 ball hit at a high trajectory

    f. 1 ball hit at a normal trajectory

Your Score =

    a. (#) _____ hit at low trajectory   d. (#) _____ hit at low trajectory

    b. (#) _____ hit at normal trajectory   e. (#) _____ hit at high trajectory

    c. (#) _____ hit at high trajectory   f. (#) _____ hit at normal trajectory

2. High-Low Drill, Alternating Odd Numbered Clubs

Repeat the High-Low Drill, but alternate clubs. This will provide a more visual contrast in trajectory control. Be sure you make your trajectory adjustments by adjusting the ball position.
Variation: Repeat this drill with your woods.

Success Goal = Hit 36 total balls, varying clubs and trajectories

    a. 9 balls (3 each at low, normal, and high trajectories) hit with a 5-iron

    b. 9 balls (3 each at low, normal, and high trajectories) hit with a 7-iron

    c. 9 balls (3 each at low, normal, and high trajectories) hit with a 9-iron

    d. 3 balls (1 each at a low trajectory with a 5-iron, 7-iron, and 9-iron)

    e. 3 balls (1 each at a normal trajectory with a 5-iron, 7-iron, and 9-iron)

    f. 3 balls (1 each at a high trajectory with a 5-iron, 7-iron, and 9-iron)

Your Score =

a. (#) _____ successful hits

b. (#) _____ successful hits

c. (#) _____ successful hits

d. (#) _____ successful hits

e. (#) _____ successful hits

f. (#) _____ successful hits

3. High-Low Drill, Alternating Successive Clubs

Repeat the High-Low Drill, alternating 6-, 7-, and 8-irons. This will help you distinguish more subtle differences in trajectory control. Make each shot travel at a different trajectory by altering the ball position.

Variation: Repeat this drill with your woods.

Success Goal = 36 total balls, alternating successive clubs

a. 9 hits (3 each at a low trajectory with 6-, 7-, and 8-iron)

b. 9 hits (3 each at a normal trajectory with 6-, 7-, and 8-iron)

c. 9 hits (3 each at a high trajectory with 6-, 7-, and 8-iron)

d. 3 hits (1 each at a low trajectory with 6-, 7-, and 8-iron)

e. 3 hits (1 each at a normal trajectory with 6-, 7-, and 8-iron)

f. 3 hits (1 each at a high trajectory with 6-, 7-, and 8-iron)

Your Score =

a. (#) _____ successful hits

b. (#) _____ successful hits

c. (#) _____ successful hits

d. (#) _____ successful hits

e. (#) _____ successful hits

f. (#) _____ successful hits

4. Grip Pressure Slice and Hook Drill

By adjusting the angle at which the clubface contacts the ball, make the ball either hook or slice. For a hook, use a light (not loose) grip pressure to cause the clubface to be closed at impact. For a slice, use increased tension in your hands and wrists, which prevents the clubhead from returning to square. This absence of wrist action keeps the clubhead open at contact.

Don't confuse the directional errors of a push or pull with the desired curvature of hooks and slices. Be sure to practice the curvature drills with both woods and irons.

Success Goal = Hit 27 total shots with a 5-iron, varying among slices, hooks, and straight shots by adjusting the angle of clubface-ball contact

a. 15 hits (5 each of slice, hook, and straight shots)

b. 9 hits (3 each of slice, hook, and straight shots)

c. 3 hits (1 each of slice, hook, and straight shots)

Your Score =

a. (#) _____ successful hits

b. (#) _____ successful hits

c. (#) _____ successful hits

5. *Grip Position Slice and Hook Drill*

You can control curvature by changing your grip position. A strong grip position helps create a hook, a weak one creates a slice, and a neutral grip creates a straight shot to a slight draw. Review Figure 2.4, a-c, for the desired grip positions of both the target and the rear hand.

Success Goal = Hit a total of 27 shots with a 6-iron, varying among slices, hooks, and straight shots by adjusting your grip position

a. 15 hits (5 each of slice, hook, and straight shots)

b. 9 hits (3 each of slice, hook, and straight shots)

c. 3 hits (1 each of slice, hook, and straight shots)

Your Score =

a. (#) _____ successful hits

b. (#) _____ successful hits

c. (#) _____ successful hits

6. *High-Low Trajectory Combined With Hook-Slice Control Drill*

You will need to be able to execute trajectory and curvature control together as well as independently, so this drill combines your previous practice on both. Through practice you will be able to control curvature more easily and consistently using either the grip pressure or the grip change method or a combination. In this drill, use the method that gives you the most dependable results at present. Remember, you can alter trajectory by modifying your ball position.

Success Goal = Hit 36 total shots with the club of your choice, combining high-low trajectories and hook-slice curvatures using the grip pressure, grip change, or combination method

a. 9 hits (3 each of high slices, hooks, and straight shots)

b. 9 hits (3 each of low slices, hooks, and straight shots)

c. 9 hits (3 each of normal slices, hooks, and straight shots)

d. 3 hits (1 each of high slice, hook, and straight shots)

e. 3 hits (1 each of low slice, hook, and straight shots)

f. 3 hits (straight shots)

Your Score =

a. (#) _____ successful hits

b. (#) _____ successful hits

c. (#) _____ successful hits

d. (#) _____ successful hits

e. (#) _____ successful hits

f. (#) _____ successful hits

7. On-Course Ball Flight Drill

Applying ball flight control on the course can be very rewarding and improve your score. But trying advanced shots without adequate practice may result in disaster. Be sure to practice the shots in these drills just like you do your regular shots. Developing confidence on advanced shots is very important. Doubting your ability to execute an intentional hook or slice out of trouble and still attempting to hit one can be more costly than chipping out to safety and going from there.

Visualize yourself in the following course situations and respond to the questions asked.

Situation A:

You're playing a par 4, 355-yard hole. The pin is tucked on the left side of the green and you're approaching from the right side of the fairway with a poor lie. You have 130 yards to the green.

a   130 yards to green

Success Goal = Respond to each question for Situation A

1. What is your best shot option?

2. What is your normal ball flight tendency?

3. What club would you use for the option in Question 1?

4. Identify your desired landing zone by shading it in.

Your Score = Answers to the questions

1. Shot option: _____

2. Your normal ball flight: _____

3. Club selection to match option: _____

4. Shading of desired landing zone on green

Situation B:

Your ball has landed 15 yards from the green, with no hazards between the two. The pin is 10 yards from the near edge of the green.

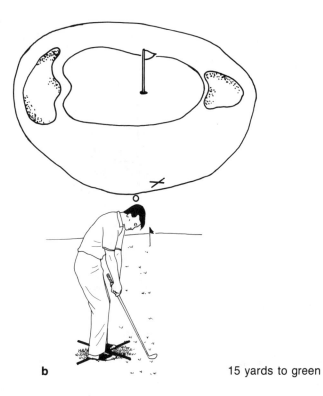

b   15 yards to green

Success Goal = Respond to each question for Situation B

1. What are your shot options?

2. What club would you use for each option?

3. Indicate your preferred shot.

Your Score = Answers to the questions

1. Shot options:

   a. _____

   b. _____

2. Club selections to match options:

   a. _____

   b. _____

3. Preferred shot: _____

Situation C:

Your second shot has landed in the woods, on the right. You are behind a willow tree with very low-hanging limbs. You are 125 yards from the green with no hazards in front.

c   125 yards to green

Success Goal = Respond to each question for Situation C

  1. What are your shot options?

  2. What club would you use for each option?

  3. Indicate your preferred shot.

Your Score = Answers to the questions

  1. Shot options:

    a. _____

    b. _____

    c. _____

  2. Club selections to match options:

    a. _____

    b. _____

    c. _____

  3. Preferred shot: _____

8. Imaginary Course Ball Flight Drill

On the practice tee, you will visualize course situations requiring you to alter your ball flight, such as a hole with a dogleg left. On that hole, you would want to hit a slight draw from the tee to gain extra yardage hitting around the dogleg. Now hit the shot you've visualized. How effective are you in hitting draws and fades?

Success Goal = Visualize 5 different course situations requiring you to alter your normal ball flight; execute the shots

    a. Over a tree

    b. Under a branch

    c. A slice around a tree

    d. A high hook over and around a tree

    e. Around a dogleg from the tee

Your Score = Success in doing the specified shots

    a. (✔) _____ Over a tree

    b. (✔) _____ Under a branch

    c. (✔) _____ Slice around a tree

    d. (✔) _____ A high hook

    e. (✔) _____ Around a dogleg

9. Bogey Golf for Ball Flight

With a partner, play a game of Bogey Golf (see Step 1, Drill 4). Try to combine changes in trajectory with changes in curvature (draws, fades, hooks, and slices).

Success Goal = Hit difficult shots that your partner cannot duplicate; duplicate partner's shots

Your Score = _____ letters earned toward "bogey"

Controlling Ball Flight
Keys to Success Checklists

Being able to control the flight of your golf ball will help you deal with the subtleties of the game. Excellent golfers can fade and draw their balls at will. Use the items in Figures 2.3 and 2.5 as checklists to evaluate your ability to control ball flight.

Answers to Drill 7

Situation A

1. Shot option
   A lower than normal trajectory from a bad lie.
2. Answer varies with the player.
3. Select a club to accommodate the lie first, distance second. If you use a club longer than a 6-iron, you need more loft to accommodate the poor lie.
4. Center area of the green shaded.

Situation B

1. Shot options

   a. Chip shot
   b. Pitch and run

2. Club selection

   a. For a chip shot, a pitching or sand wedge

b. For a pitch and run, a pitching or sand wedge (so the ball will not run as far as with a 6-iron)

Situation C

1. Shot options

   a. Low back into the fairway
   b. Low slice (if right-handed; very difficult, but possible)
   c. Low hook (if left-handed)

2. Club selection

   a. 3- or 4-iron
   b. 3-iron (because opening the clubface to produce the slice adds loft)
   c. 4-iron (because closing the clubface to produce the hook removes loft)

Step 3   Controlling Distance

During your early practice sessions and on the course, you may have felt that your ball went about the same distance with every club. Or perhaps you hit longer with your short irons (7,8,9) than your long ones (3,4,5,6). But as your swing improved, so did your distance with each club. Without our going into the aerodynamics of ball flight, suffice it to say that with practice you both increased your clubhead speed and improved your ability to consistently contact the ball below the center. Both factors are critical for getting the ball into the air and creating greater distance and consistency.

WHY IS CONTROLLING DISTANCE IMPORTANT?

As you approach the green you need greater precision in controlling the distance the ball goes as well as the direction. From the tee to the green, your target area goes from wide to narrow (see Figure 3.1). Your tee shot can tolerate a greater range in direction and distance because the target area is longer and wider. The target area of the green is smaller and narrower than the fairway, and you're going for an even smaller area on the green near the pin. You might hit a great shot with ideal trajectory and right on line to your target but far too long or short. Misjudging distance can cost you many shots during a round.

HOW TO EXECUTE DISTANCE CONTROL

You may be surprised to learn that the difference in distance for the average golfer between clubs is only about 8 yards (plus or minus 3). So if you hit about 135 yards with your 5-iron, your 6-iron should take you between 124 and 130 yards. Even the pros only create differences of 12 or 13 yards, plus or minus 3. With practice on the following drills, you will be able to better judge your distance with each club.

Developing good distance control requires that you (1) determine the distance to the pin; (2) select the appropriate club; and (3) make the right swing motion.

Determine the Distance to the Pin

Judging distance combines visual training, experience, and luck (yes, luck!). With systematic practice you can train yourself to judge distance. For example, you can go to a football field and use the yardage lines to practice identifying various distances. By paying more attention to the distances you hit in practice (noting how far each ball travels in the air and on the ground), you will be able to incorporate this awareness and experience into your course play.

On the course, luck is always a factor. Greens vary; you can hit a perfect shot to the green—trajectory, direction, and distance just as

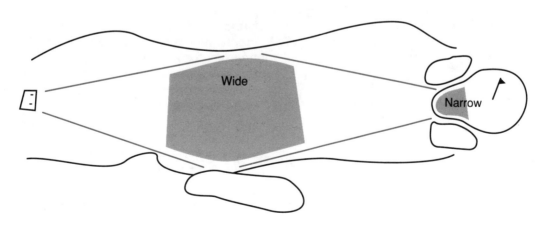

Figure 3.1 The target area goes from wide to narrow from the tee to the green.

planned—but the ball might hit a hard spot that sends it bouncing over the green or a soft one that causes it to stop short. These things happen, and they're out of your control—so don't waste energy worrying about those ''bad bounces.''

Today's courses provide yardage markers (posts, bushes, fairway discs, markings on sprinkler heads, etc.) to denote distances of 150 and 100 yards from the green. Some even mark 200 and 50 yards. (Additional yardage aids may be on the scorecard or in yardage books that are more precise but cost more money). When you sign up to play, ask about any yardage markers on the course.

The Controlling Distance Keys to Success Checklist (at the end of this step) provides experiences for visual training and for walking off distances. Practice these frequently for reinforcement and to check your judgment.

Select the Appropriate Club

Club selection is determined by your best estimate of the distance you want, considering both distance in the air (air time) and distance on the ground (ground time). Let's imagine two situations (see Figure 3.2, a and b). From ball to pin is 150 yards. In Figure 3.2a, the area between them is unobstructed. But in Figure 3.2b, there is a trap. To the top of trap is 135 yards, and from the trap to the pin is 15. Would you use the same club for both situations?

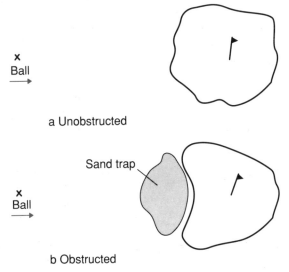

Figure 3.2 Situations in club selection.

Well, on the practice tee you consistently hit your 4-iron between 145 and 155 yards, and you've noted that the air time is between 135

and 140 yards. So you may be thinking a 4-iron would be fine for both situations. Not quite. It would be suitable for the shot without the trap, but you'd be cutting it pretty close going over the trap. A slight miss and your ball will be buried in the sand. The 3-iron or 5-wood would give you a larger margin of error. Better to land on the green beyond the pin and putt than to end up in the trap.

Terrain is another consideration in club selection. Note the three situations in Figure 3.3, a-c (level terrain versus the elevated and downhill greens). The yardage in each case is 130.

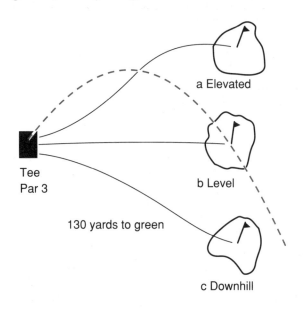

Figure 3.3 For an elevated tee, select a longer club (a); for a normal tee, select the standard club for that distance (b); and for a downhill green, select a shorter club to avoid hitting beyond the green (c).

To get to the level green, the club you hit for 125 to 135 yards would be appropriate. But that club would land your ball short on the elevated green and long on the downhill green. There is no exact formula for gauging which club to hit for differences in terrain. But for a start, hit one club more (for uphill) or less (for downhill) for each 10-yard change in elevation. Note the results when you change clubs, and apply your observations to future situations.

It is important to know the average distances you hit your clubs. At times you'll be the longest hitter in a group, at times the shortest. Don't let ego interfere with your performance: The key is to get the ball to the target with whatever club it takes. Choose your shots and your clubs based on *your* ability, not someone else's. Learning this early will make you a better player.

Although there are no given distances that every player should be able to hit the ball, Table 3.1 lists some averages for men and women hitting with various clubs. Shorter and longer hitters may differ by 15 to 30 yards less or more.

Table 3.1 Average Distances Hit With Various Clubs

| Club | Distance in yards | |
	Men	Women
Driver	235	190
3-wood	220	180
4-wood	210	170
5-wood	200	160
7-wood	*	150
2-iron	190	*
3-iron	180	155
4-iron	170	145
5-iron	160	135
6-iron	150	125
7-iron	140	115
8-iron	130	105
9-iron	120	95
Pitching wedge	110	80
Sand wedge	80	50
Lofted wedge	40	*

*Indicates clubs often not carried, so no average distance is given.

We hope by now you understand that selecting the appropriate club is not guesswork. To help you develop a systematic strategy for selecting clubs, a checklist is provided at the end of this step (see the Controlling Distance Keys to Success Checklist).

Make the Right Swing Motion

Your swing motion controls distance because it influences the speed and length of your swing. For your full swing, you want a pace you can control and repeat consistently (usually between 65 and 80 percent of your potential maximum).

Swing speed is the measured speed of the swing on the forwardswing, through impact. The backswing is slower, with the forwardswing developing acceleration as the swing changes direction through the weight shift and the arms, hands, and club start down as a unit.

Your swing length can be short of parallel, or parallel, or just beyond parallel, as illustrated in Figure 3.4, a-c. Developing consistency in both

a Beyond parallel

b Short of parallel   c Parallel

Figure 3.4 Variations of swing lengths.

swing pace and length is critical to selecting clubs and knowing your distances for each.

When a full swing with your 9-iron would send the ball too far, you must begin making partial shots. Partial, or short approach, shots include pitch shots, chip shots, and some sand shots. Distance control is more of a challenge because of the great variation in distances required. To hit short approach shots effectively, you must select the right swing pace and length for distances anywhere from 4 to 90 yards. The swing pace varies from moderately fast to slow, and swing lengths from 1 to 5 (illustrated in Figure 3.5, a-f; a full swing would be a 4 or 5).

Most golfers more readily duplicate the 5 swing length than Lengths 1 through 4, which typically require greater practice relative to distance control.

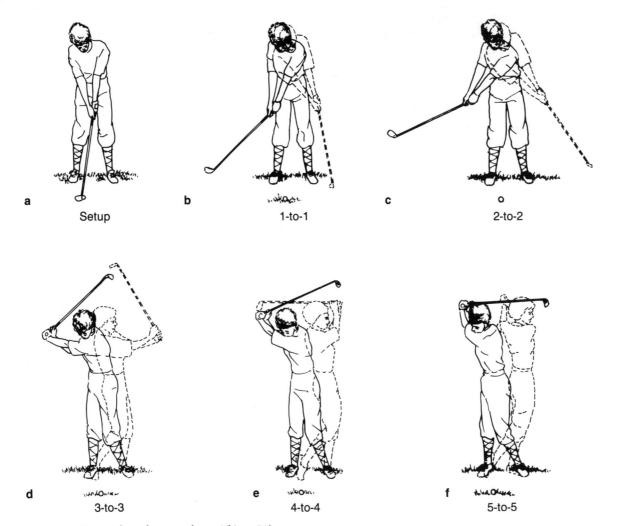

Figure 3.5 Swing lengths vary from 1(b) to 5(f).

The drills in this step will help you focus on a combination of swing length and pace control to regulate your distances.

On the practice tee and the course, consistently evaluate your distance results based on your attempted swing length and pace.

Detecting Distance Control Errors

When evaluating your errors in distance, begin by asking three questions: How accurate was your estimate of distance? Did you choose the right club? Did you use the appropriate swing pace and swing length? By pinpointing errors in any of the three areas, you can direct your practice sessions more effectively.

ERROR	CORRECTION
1. The designated target was 130 yards on a par 3. Your ball carried 15 yards over the target.	1. Recheck your club distances for 130 yards. You may have selected the wrong club.
2. Your 40-yard pitch shots land consistently short of the target.	2. Use a mirror to check that your swing length is not too short. Take the desired swing, but stop at the end of the backswing and check the position of the club. Then hit balls 40 yards, working on the swing length and swing pace. If shots are still short, lengthen your swing.
3. Full shots with an 8-iron are erratic in distance.	3. Practice your pace control using Drill 3. Note the distances and consistency in control.
4. Shots on the course with the 5-iron land short of the target.	4. Hit 10 to 20 shots on the practice tee. Walk off the distance to the average length of the shots. How close is this to what you hit on the course? You may need to adjust your average distance for 5-iron shots.

Drills for Controlling Distance

1. Distance Assessment Drill With Irons

This drill will help you assess your current distance with each iron. Your ideal is to hit the ball as far as you can with consistent control of distance and predictable trajectory, using your normal swing for each club. On a practice range it is difficult to predict roll, so focus on the average distance (carry) your ball gets while in the air. As you play, you will learn to judge the amount of roll more accurately.

Place eight or more targets in a field at 10-yard intervals, beginning 100 yards from the ball.

Starting with a 5-iron, practice hitting balls toward the targets. Use an alignment club to assure direction, and take your setup position carefully with each swing. Determine the average distance you hit your 5-iron by noting the distance of the majority of shots. Continue this process with each iron. You may need to adjust your yardage markers to fit your distance needs. (To avoid inaccuracies on account of fatigue, you may want to take 2 or more days to assess your distance with all your irons.)

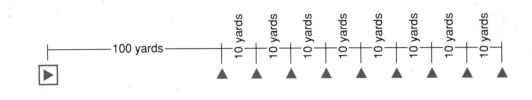

Success Goal = Hit consistent distance 80 percent or better

a. 10 hits with a 5-iron

b. 10 hits with a 6-iron

c. 10 hits with a 3-iron

d. 10 hits with a 7-iron

e. 10 hits with a 4-iron

f. 10 hits with an 8-iron

g. 10 hits with a 9-iron

h. 10 hits with a pitching wedge

i. 10 hits with a sand wedge

Your Score = Distance hit (hit all 10 shots with each club in the order given)

Shot	Irons								
	5	6	3	7	4	8	9	PW	SW
1	___	___	___	___	___	___	___	___	___
2	___	___	___	___	___	___	___	___	___
3	___	___	___	___	___	___	___	___	___
4	___	___	___	___	___	___	___	___	___
5	___	___	___	___	___	___	___	___	___
6	___	___	___	___	___	___	___	___	___
7	___	___	___	___	___	___	___	___	___
8	___	___	___	___	___	___	___	___	___
9	___	___	___	___	___	___	___	___	___
10	___	___	___	___	___	___	___	___	___
Total	___	___	___	___	___	___	___	___	___
Average	___	___	___	___	___	___	___	___	___

2. Distance Assessment Drill With Woods

Repeat Drill 1 using your woods, adjusting the markers for your distance before beginning this drill. It is best to do Drills 1 and 2 on different days. (*Note:* Not all golfers carry five different woods. Do this drill with whatever woods you carry.)

Success Goal = Hit consistent distance 80 percent or better

a. 10 hits with a 7-wood

b. 10 hits with a 3-wood

c. 10 hits with a driver

d. 10 hits with a 4-wood

e. 10 hits with a 5-wood

Your Score = Distance hit (hit all 10 shots with each club in the order given)

Shot	7	3	Woods Driver	4	5
1	___	___	___	___	___
2	___	___	___	___	___
3	___	___	___	___	___
4	___	___	___	___	___
5	___	___	___	___	___
6	___	___	___	___	___
7	___	___	___	___	___
8	___	___	___	___	___
9	___	___	___	___	___
10	___	___	___	___	___
Total	___	___	___	___	___
Average	___	___	___	___	___

3. Swing Pace Drill

Drills 1 and 2 have helped you assess your average distance with each club using your normal swing speed or pace (65 to 80 percent of maximum). Conditions on the course, though, often require shots at less or more than your normal swing speed. For example, you might find yourself in a situation where your normal swing speed for a 5-iron would go too far, and you would have to force your 6-iron to go the distance because there's a trap in front. This drill will help you learn to control distance through the pace of your swing. Use the same distance targets you set up in Drills 1 and 2.

Success Goal = Hit 50 total shots, varying the club and swing pace

a. 6-iron

    5 hits at normal pace

    5 hits at 1/2 normal pace

    5 hits at normal pace

    5 hits at 1/2 normal pace

    5 hits at normal pace

b. 4-wood (or your choice)

    5 hits at normal pace

    5 hits at 1/2 normal pace

    5 hits at normal pace

    5 hits at 1/2 normal pace

    5 hits at normal pace

Your Score = Distance hit

Pace	Hits						
	1	2	3	4	5	Total	Average
a. 6-Iron							
Normal	___	___	___	___	___	___	___
1/2	___	___	___	___	___	___	___
Normal	___	___	___	___	___	___	___
1/2	___	___	___	___	___	___	___
Normal	___	___	___	___	___	___	___
b. 4-Wood							
Normal	___	___	___	___	___	___	___
1/2	___	___	___	___	___	___	___
Normal	___	___	___	___	___	___	___
1/2	___	___	___	___	___	___	___
Normal	___	___	___	___	___	___	___

4. Swing Length Drill

Swing length is another means of controlling distance. For full swing shots, a shorter swing length (a 4 swing length rather than a 5) will reduce your distance. Practice this drill using your normal swing pace (as practiced in Drill 3). Note the differences in distance that result by varying clubs and swing length.

Success Goal = Hit 30 total shots using your normal swing pace

a. 7-iron

5 hits with a normal swing length

5 hits with a 4 swing length

5 hits with a normal swing length

b. 9-iron

5 hits with a normal swing length

5 hits with a 4 swing length

5 hits with a normal swing length

Your Score = Distance hit

Length	Swings						
	1	2	3	4	5	Total	Average
a. 7-Iron							
Normal	___	___	___	___	___	___	___
4	___	___	___	___	___	___	___
Normal	___	___	___	___	___	___	___

Length	Swings					Total	Average
	1	2	3	4	5		
b. 9-iron							
Normal	____	____	____	____	____	____	____
4	____	____	____	____	____	____	____
Normal	____	____	____	____	____	____	____

5. Pace and Swing Length Drill

A third way of controlling distance is to combine alterations in swing length and swing pace. For this drill, note the changes in distance that result from various combinations.

Success Goal = Hit 21 total shots using a 7-iron (or your choice)

  a. 3 hits with normal swing length and pace

  b. 3 hits with 4 swing length and 1/2 normal pace

  c. 2 hits with normal swing length and pace

  d. 2 hits with normal swing length and 1/2 normal pace

  e. 2 hits with normal swing length and pace

  f. 3 hits with 4 swing length and normal pace

  g. 2 hits with normal swing length and pace

  h. 3 hits with normal swing length and 1/2 normal pace

  i. 1 hit with normal swing length and pace

Your Score = Distance hit

Swing length/Swing pace	Shots		
	1	2	3
a. Normal length and pace	____	____	____
b. 4 length, 1/2 pace	____	____	____
c. Normal length and pace	____	____	
d. Normal length, 1/2 pace	____	____	
e. Normal length and pace	____	____	
f. 4 length, normal pace	____	____	____
g. Normal length and pace	____	____	
h. Normal length, 1/2 pace	____	____	____
i. Normal length and pace	____		

6. Judging Distance Drill

Distance judgment improves through visual practice and experience. This drill provides a way to check your distances when you practice judging them on a course in Drill 7. At a local soccer or football field, sit on an end line and focus on different distances (10 yards, 40 yards, 70 yards, etc.). Take visual pictures of the various distances, then walk them off. How does your normal stride length compare to the marked yardage? Repeat this several times, feeling the distance as you walk it. Repeat this drill as often as you can; the better you can judge distance, the better you'll be able to select the best club for your game.

Success Goal = 10 trips to a soccer or football field with active visual study and walking distances

Your Score = (#) _____ trips to a soccer or football field for active visual study and walking distances; place a checkmark each time you visit the field and complete this drill. Also, note the number of strides it takes to pace off 10 yards

	Trips									
	1	2	3	4	5	6	7	8	9	10
Visual study	___	___	___	___	___	___	___	___	___	___
Walking distance	___	___	___	___	___	___	___	___	___	___
# of strides in 10 yards	___	___	___	___	___	___	___	___	___	___

7. Course Practice for Judging Distance

Continual practice on judging distance is imperative to improving your scoring average. On the course, select an object (tree, hazard, etc.) in the distance, and predict its distance. Then walk off the distance to your object to check your accuracy.

Success Goal = 90 percent accuracy (within 5 yards short or long)

Your Score = 10 attempts over 2 rounds (check off 1 of the 4 accuracy categories for each attempt)

	Accuracy			
Attempts	Within 3 yards	Within 5 yards	Within 10 yards	Off more than 10 yards
1	___	___	___	___
2	___	___	___	___
3	___	___	___	___
4	___	___	___	___
5	___	___	___	___
6	___	___	___	___
7	___	___	___	___

Accuracy

Attempts	Within 3 yards	Within 5 yards	Within 10 yards	Off more than 10 yards
8	____	____	____	____
9	____	____	____	____
10	____	____	____	____
Total	____	____	____	____
%	____	____	____	____

8. Course Practice for Club Selection

You have practiced off the course to determine your distance for each club using Drills 1 through 4. Applying this knowledge to the course combines your ability to *judge your distances* and *select the desired club*, based on the lie of the ball and the desired trajectory.

Play 18 holes, keeping track of estimated and actual distances from the hole on your approach shots, the clubs selected, and the results of your shots relative to the pin positions (i.e., short, on target, or long). Walk off the actual distance after you hit each shot. To be judged on-target, a ball must end up within 5 yards of the pin, long, short, or even ("pin high"). This will help you determine your strengths and weaknesses in both areas.

Success Goal = Keep track of each approach shot during 18 holes

Your Score = Record your yardages, lies, and results

Hole	Distance		Lie	Club selection	Results
	Estimated	Actual	Poor/ Good		Short, On target, Long
Example	85	95	Poor	9-i	Short
1	____	____	____	____	____
2	____	____	____	____	____
3	____	____	____	____	____
4	____	____	____	____	____
5	____	____	____	____	____
6	____	____	____	____	____
7	____	____	____	____	____
8	____	____	____	____	____
9	____	____	____	____	____
10	____	____	____	____	____
11	____	____	____	____	____

Hole	Distance		Lie	Club selection	Results
	Estimated	Actual	Poor/ Good		Short, On target, Long
12	____	____	____	____	____
13	____	____	____	____	____
14	____	____	____	____	____
15	____	____	____	____	____
16	____	____	____	____	____
17	____	____	____	____	____
18	____	____	____	____	____
Total	____	____	____	____	____

After completing the round, answer the following questions:

1. How well do you select clubs? Do you tend to underestimate or overestimate your driving distance?
2. How does the lie of the ball affect the shot? Distance? Trajectory?
3. If your shot was too short or too long, what caused the error? Inaccurate yardage estimates? Poor club selection? Difficult lie?

Controlling Distance Keys to Success Checklist

Controlling distance comes from practice. Through systematic practice in judging distance, visual training, and knowledge of the distance you hit each club, your course play will improve. The experiences in the following checklist will help you add greater consistency to your distance judgments and consequently help you make better club selections during play.

You can use this checklist in several ways. Initially, you may want to review the considerations for club selection before your round and literally check off each item as it is executed. After you feel more comfortable on the course, blend all this strategy information into your play by using the checklist as a quick mental review—checking yourself at random against the actual checklist items. Even tour professionals have their own ''checklists.''

Note that terrain and weather have been included as considerations on this checklist. These will be discussed in greater detail in Steps 4 and 9, respectively. Both are important elements in your strategy development.

Determine Distance

Practice distance judging
  a. Visual training
     At a football field ____
     At a soccer field ____
     At a baseball diamond ____
  b. Walk off distances
     During course play ____
     On the street ____
     At school ____
     In the park ____

Identify your number of natural strides for 10 yards
   Number of strides in 10 yards ____
Inquire regarding distance markers
   In your practice area ____
   On courses played ____

Select the Appropriate Club

Determine lie of the ball ____
Determine the trajectory ____
Determine distance to target
   Distance in the air ____
   Distance of expected roll ____
Consider obstacles
   Traps ____
   Water hazards ____
   Out of bounds ____
   Trees, bushes ____
Consider weather
   Wind ____
   Rain ____
Consider terrain
   Flat ____
   Hilly ____
   Undulating ____

Select Swing Motion

Determine swing length
   1 ____
   2 ____
   3 ____
   4 ____
   5 ____
Determine swing pace
   Slow ____
   Normal ____
   Moderately fast ____

Evaluate Results

Shot distance
   Appropriate ____
   Long ____
   Short ____

Step 4 **Variations in Pitch Shots**

The pitch shot is one of the shots most frequently used from less than 100 yards to the green. Earlier in your golf career, your objective was simply to get on the green "somewhere" when you were that close. The objective now is to "get close." We will review the basic pitch shot and introduce you to two variations, the lob shot, for higher trajectory, and the pitch and run shot, for lower trajectory. The basic pitch trajectory is between the lob and the pitch and run. The three trajectories are illustrated in Figure 4.1, a-c.

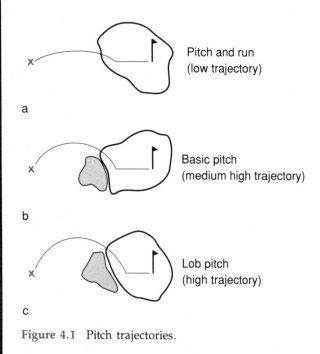

Figure 4.1 Pitch trajectories.

WHY ARE PITCH SHOT VARIATIONS IMPORTANT?

Pins are not always positioned in the middle of the green. Nor are you always the same distance from the pin or provided a good lie. You could use the basic pitch shot for all pitch situations and get on or near the green, but if you want to get closer to the pin for more one-putts or pitch-ins, the lob shot and low shots can be valuable.

Note the three situations illustrated in Figure 4.2, a-c. In each situation, the player is 30 yards from the pin. However, the situations provide

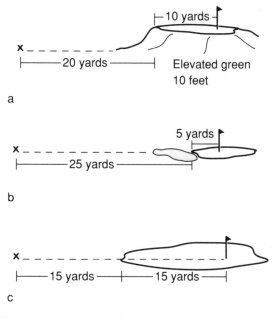

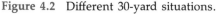

Figure 4.2 Different 30-yard situations.

different challenges for the approach shot. Consider the possible options (pitch, lob, and pitch and run) and assume the lie of the ball is good:

Situation A: The area between the ball and the pin is free of hazards or obstacles. The green is elevated about 10 feet. The ball is 20 yards from the green, and the pin is 10 yards from the near edge of the green.
Options: All three options are possible, but the *basic pitch shot* with a sand wedge is the better trajectory to choose. The lob requires more precision, and the pitch and run would be more difficult to judge with the elevated green. (Both of these will be discussed in greater detail in the section to follow.)

Situation B: There is a trap between the ball and the green. The ball is 25 yards from the green, and the pin is 5 yards from the near edge of the green.
Options: This is a tight pin placement, and it will be difficult to get the ball close, because this shot requires a high trajectory with little roll (which eliminates the pitch and run). The basic pitch shot with a sand wedge is the safest shot; it would get you on the green and putting, but

not necessarily close to the pin. The lob has the greatest chance of getting close to the pin, but it is more difficult because its execution requires such precision. The basic pitch will require fewer swing adjustments.

Situation C: The approach to the green is clear and level rather than elevated. The ball is 15 yards from the green, and the pin is 15 yards from the near edge of the green.
Options: All three shot options are usable in this situation. The best option is the *pitch and run* with an 8- or 9-iron. This is the safest and most predictable shot, given the level surface and the 15 yards to run the ball on the green.

Once you begin to understand the three types of pitch shots, you'll learn to apply them appropriately by practicing on the course. Let's focus now on how to execute the shots.

HOW TO EXECUTE PITCH SHOT VARIATIONS

The pitch shot is executed with a partial swing, used to go a shorter distance than normal for that club. It has more air time than ground time. Depending on the distance required, your swing length and swing pace may vary. The swing length varies from 3 to 4 for the basic pitch and the lob shots, and from 2 to 3 with the pitch and run shot (review Figure 3.5). The swing pace varies from slow to moderately fast. The pitching wedge (PW) and the sand wedge (SW) are used most frequently for the basic pitch shot and the lob shot. The pitch and run can be used with any club, but generally with anything from a 6-iron through the sand wedge.

Basic Pitch

The basic pitch shot swing is similar to the full swing motion, but it has a shorter length and a more vertical path to create a higher trajectory. The modified setup position uses a neutral grip and square clubface. The stance is slightly open in your feet (which are slightly less than shoulder-width apart), with square hips and shoulders. Your weight is even between both feet and carried between the instep and the balls of the feet. The ball position is slightly forward of center in your stance (see center column in Figure 4.3).

The swing motion of the basic pitch is a half to three-quarters swing, in a pendular motion with the backswing and forwardswing equal, with a swing length of 3-to-3 or 4-to-4. Your weight shifts slightly in response to the arm swing in both the backswing and the forward-swing. Your wrist cocks on the backswing and uncocks and recocks on the forwardswing. The pitch swing motion is illustrated in the center column of Figure 4.3.

Lob Pitch

The lob pitch is a high, soft shot used to go short distances (30 to 40 yards). Generally it is a low-percentage shot, because most players must put in a lot of practice to use it effectively. As such, it is the most misused shot around the green. We present it because when you use the lob in appropriate situations, as your skill improves, it can save you shots. On the other hand, misused, it can be costly to your score. Use the lob sparingly and only where height and very little roll are major factors—for instance, when you must go over a trap to a pin near the trap side of the green with very little green on which to land the ball.

The setup position and swing motion for the lob are slightly modified from the basic pitch shot to create the high, softer trajectory with little roll. For your setup, use your neutral grip, but open the face slightly before taking your grip (see the left column in Figure 4.3). Your shoulders and hips are open with your feet.

In the swing motion, the swing arc is steeper or more upright than in the basic pitch shot, with a minimum swing length of 4. This is a result of the open position of your shoulders and hips and the need to create both height and distance. When height is added to the ball trajectory, distance will be less. Therefore, you need a longer swing length.

Modify your forwardswing by reducing your wrist motion. Do not recock your wrist after impact. Keep the clubface open throughout the swing. You will feel as though the club is sliding under the ball. The swing motion is smooth and rhythmical (see the left column in Figure 4.3).

The sand wedge is easier to use for the lob than the pitching wedge because it has more loft. Manufacturers have developed wedges with more loft than the sand wedge; these ''lob wedges'' or ''third wedges'' are ideal for this shot but not a necessity.

Pitch and Run Shot

The pitch and run is a low shot. It is a high-percentage shot compared to the lob pitch, because it is easier to control and reproduce consistently. The pitch and run is an in-between shot, blending the pitch and chip shots, that is used when your basic pitch would go too far or you are too far out to chip.

The pitch and run shot has two setup modifications from the basic pitch shot. The ball is positioned just back of center toward your rear foot. This helps to create a lower ball trajectory. Your weight is more on the target side rather than evenly distributed on both feet—about 60 percent of your weight leaning toward the target side, with about 40 percent on the rear side (see the right column in Figure 4.3).

The swing motion of the pitch and run has three changes from the basic pitch. The swing length varies from 2 for short shots to 3 for longer shots. However, this shot is not designed for long distances. There is wrist motion on the backswing with a restricted wrist movement on the forwardswing (see the right column in Figure 4.3). A light grip pressure will help you feel the club during the swing. The clubface remains square to the target. With your weight positioned more toward the target side, you will have some motion in your lower body, though less than in the basic pitch. Allow your lower body to respond to the arm swing.

The pitch and run shot is also a good stroke saver when you are recovering from an errant shot into the woods or under bushes. Practice with a variety of clubs and notice the differences in trajectory control.

Figure 4.3 Keys to Success: *Pitch Shots*

(*indicates variation from basic pitch shot)

**Preparation
Phase**

Setup

Lob Pitch

a

1. Neutral grip ____
2. Feet closer than shoulder-width apart ____

Basic Pitch

a

1. Neutral grip ____
2. Feet closer than shoulder-width apart ____

Pitch and Run

a

1. Neutral grip ____
2. Feet closer than shoulder-width apart ____

Lob Pitch	*Basic Pitch*	*Pitch and Run*
3. Weight even ____	3. Weight even ____	*3. Weight target side ____
4. Alignment	4. Alignment	4. Alignment
a. Feet slightly open ____	a. Feet slightly open ____	a. Feet slightly open ____
*b. Hips slightly open ____	b. Hips square ____	b. Hips square ____
*c. Shoulders slightly open ____	c. Shoulders parallel to target ____	c. Shoulders parallel to target ____
5. Posture with flat back ____	5. Posture with flat back ____	5. Posture with flat back ____
6. Arms relaxed and hanging ____	6. Arms relaxed and hanging ____	6. Arms relaxed and hanging ____
7. Weight instep to balls of feet ____	7. Weight instep to balls of feet ____	7. Weight instep to balls of feet ____
8. Ball position: Forward of center ____	8. Ball position: Forward of center ____	*8. Ball position: Back of center ____
*9. Blade position: Open ____	9. Blade position: Square ____	*9. Blade position: Square, but deflofted ____

**Execution
Phase**

Backswing

Lob Pitch	*Basic Pitch*	*Pitch and Run*

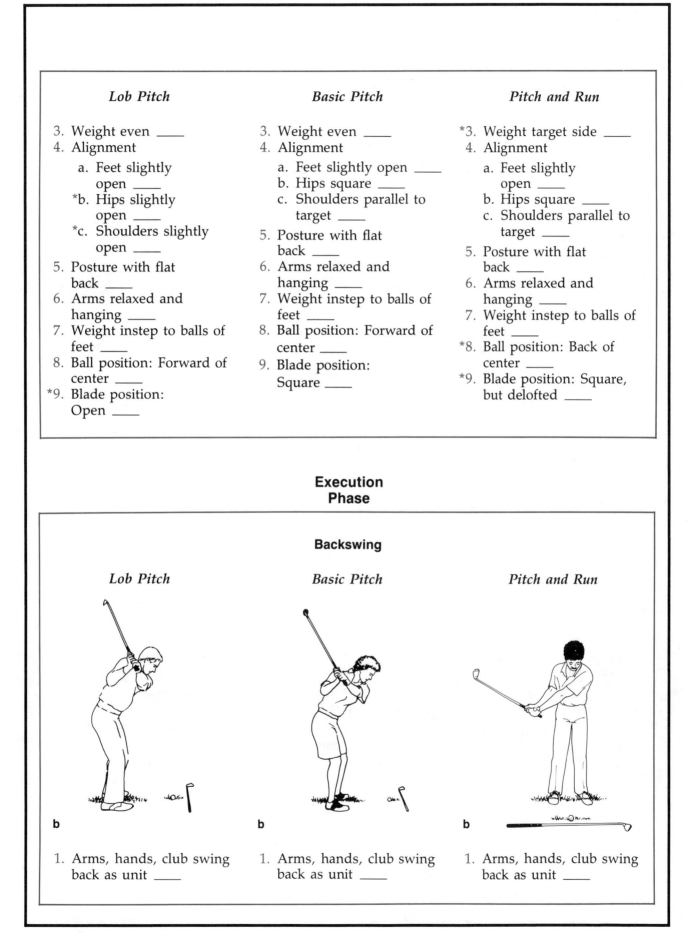

b	b	b
1. Arms, hands, club swing back as unit ____	1. Arms, hands, club swing back as unit ____	1. Arms, hands, club swing back as unit ____

Lob Pitch	*Basic Pitch*	*Pitch and Run*

Lob Pitch

2. Weight shift: Back to rear ____
3. Wrist cock: By hip level ____
4. Hip turn (approximately 45°) ____
5. Backswing length:
   3 ____
   4 ____
6. Heel of target foot: Slightly off ground ____
7. Shoulder turn: Approximately 80° to 90° ____

Basic Pitch

2. Weight shift: Back to rear ____
3. Wrist cock: By hip level ____
4. Hip turn (approximately 45°) ____
5. Backswing length:
   3 ____
   4 ____
6. Heel of target foot: Slightly off ground ____
7. Shoulder turn: Approximately 80° to 90° ____

Pitch and Run

*2. Weight shift: Slight ____ (70 percent stays on target side)
*3. Wrist cock: Before hip level ____
4. Hip turn (approximately 45° ____
5. Backswing length:
   *2 ____
   *3 ____
*6. Heel of target foot: Remains on ground ____
*7. Shoulder turn: Approximately 45° ____

Forwardswing

Lob Pitch	*Basic Pitch*	*Pitch and Run*

Lob Pitch

1. Weight shifts to target side:
   a. Target heel down ____
   b. Target knee to target ____
2. Hands, arms, club swing down as a unit ____
3. Wrists uncock at hip level ____

Basic Pitch

1. Weight shifts to target side:
   a. Target heel down ____
   b. Target knee to target ____
2. Hands, arms, club swing down as a unit ____
3. Wrists uncock at hip level ____

Pitch and Run

1. Weight shifts to target side:
   a. Target heel down ____
   b. Target knee to target ____
2. Hands, arms, club swing down as a unit ____
*3. Wrists uncock by weight of club ____

Follow-Through
Phase

Lob Pitch	*Basic Pitch*	*Pitch and Run*

d

1. Weight on target side ____
2. Hips face target ____
3. Chest to target ____
4. Forwardswing length:

   3 ____
   4 ____
5. Balanced ending ____

d

1. Weight on target side ____
2. Hips face target ____
3. Chest to target ____
4. Forwardswing length:

   3 ____
   4 ____
5. Balanced ending ____

d

1. Weight on target side ____
*2. Hips slightly face target ____
*3. Chest slightly to target ____
4. Forwardswing length:

   *2 ____
   *3 ____
5. Balanced ending ____

CONSIDERATIONS FOR SHOT SELECTION

Your first consideration in selecting a pitch shot is the lie of the ball. If the lie is good and the ball is sitting up on the grass, any shot option is possible, and you can get full distance from your club. However, if the ball is in a poor lie, such as in heavy grass or a divot or on hard bare ground, your options are reduced. Now a medium or lower trajectory is dictated (eliminating the lob shot). The distance may be limited, and the desired target may not be attainable. You must alter your stance so that the ball is rear of the center of your stance. You might also have to alter your forwardswing. For example, heavy grass may slow your club through impact in both full swing and approach shot motions.

The terrain is an additional consideration. When the ball is on an uneven surface, such as an uphill, a downhill, or a sidehill lie, as illustrated in Figure 4.4, a-d, trajectory, distance, and curvature can all be affected.

Visualizing Your Shots

On television you often hear the commentators say that a player is "visualizing the shot." This refers to determining the type of trajectory and the amount of roll that a particular situation requires and imagining how that will look. For example, visualizing a lob would involve seeing in your mind's eye (imagining) a high lob, like you see in tennis, versus a low pitch or a pitch and run, which would be much lower.

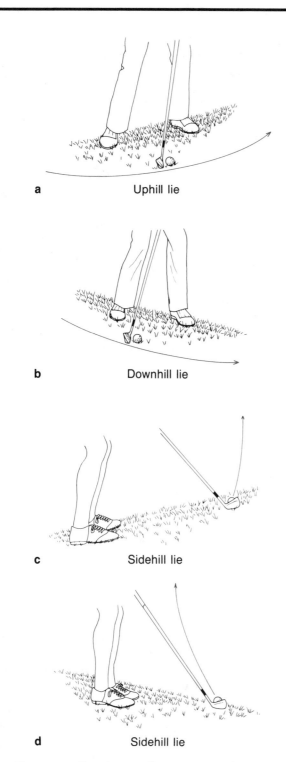

a   Uphill lie

b   Downhill lie

c   Sidehill lie

d   Sidehill lie

Figure 4.4 Terrain can effect trajectory, distance, and curvature.

By imagining the shot, you can get a free look at what the result might be. You can imagine two alternative shots, and then choose the one that feels and looks the best. Once you have evaluated your options, you can select the appropriate club to produce the desired shot.

When visualizing your shot, be sure to consider the effect of the lie of the ball as well as the desired distance. In addition, it is obviously important to consider the trajectory, as in pitching over a small tree.

As you begin practicing your pitch shot drills, be sure to practice visualizing the trajectory differences in the three types of pitch shots. Then on the course you will find that visualizing your shots is starting to come naturally.

Differences in Playing Uneven and Level Lies

The major considerations in playing uneven lies are your setup position, which must accommodate the slope, and your balance, which affects the potential swing length and swing pace. See Figure 4.5 for setup positions for uphill/downhill shots and sidehill shots when the ball is above or below your feet. Only the setup positions that differ from your normal setup are presented.

Uneven lies require setup modifications for grip, weight distribution, and alignment. The grip modification is not in hand position but in club length. Choke your grip down to shorten the club length, because you are closer to the ball. This makes it easier to swing.

For weight distribution, the key is to get yourself balanced and let common sense guide you. For example, on the sidehill lie with the ball below your feet, if you put your weight toward your toes, you will fall down the slope. Similarly for the uphill and downhill lies: With too much weight on the low foot as you swing, you will feel yourself falling toward the downslope.

Figure 4.5 Keys to Success:
Differences in Setup Position for Uneven Lies
(*indicates variation from basic setup position)

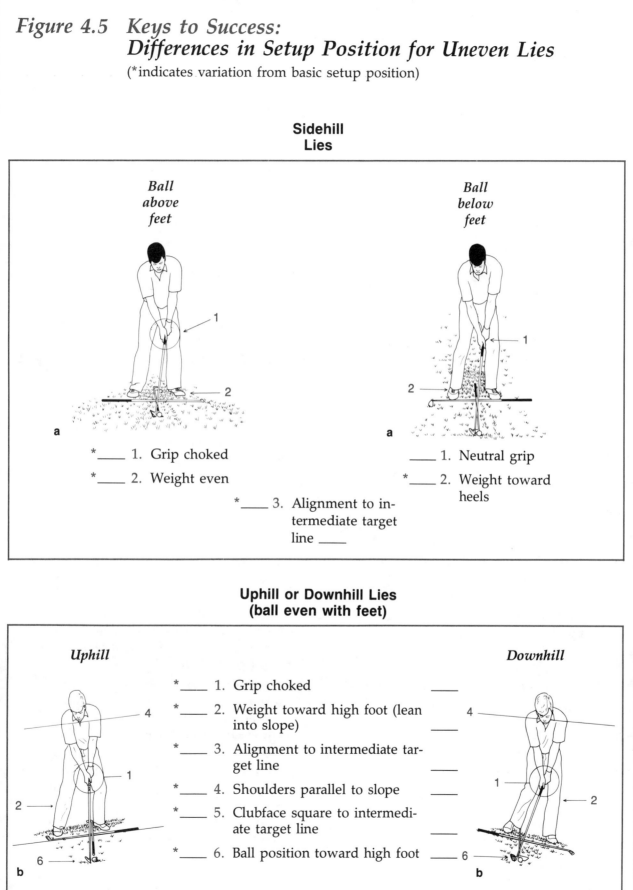

Sidehill Lies

Ball above feet

*___ 1. Grip choked

*___ 2. Weight even

___ 3. Alignment to intermediate target line ___

Ball below feet

___ 1. Neutral grip

*___ 2. Weight toward heels

Uphill or Downhill Lies
(ball even with feet)

Uphill · *Downhill*

*___ 1. Grip choked ___

*___ 2. Weight toward high foot (lean into slope) ___

*___ 3. Alignment to intermediate target line ___

*___ 4. Shoulders parallel to slope ___

*___ 5. Clubface square to intermediate target line ___

*___ 6. Ball position toward high foot ___

In both categories of uneven lies, note the alignment to the intermediate target. The slope affects swing path and clubface position at impact. Rather than a swing adjustment to counter the slope effects, it is easier to alter your alignment slightly toward an intermediate target and allow for the curvature. The more severe the slope, the greater the potential curvature. Here are the ball flight tendencies for uneven lies:

Sidehill lies	Curvature
Ball above feet	Draw
Ball below feet	Fade

Uphill/Downhill lies	Curvature
Uphill	Draw
Downhill	Fade

For uphill/downhill lies, modify the ball position by moving the ball closer to your high foot. Be sure to take practice swings to determine the low point in your swing arc.

These differences occur for *all* shots. If you play relatively flat courses, often the areas around the greens are elevated. The conditions described here pertain to short shots as well.

These setup modifications will seem awkward at first, but stick with them. With practice and course experience you will be more comfortable with them, and this will help you learn to play under all conditions.

Detecting Pitching Errors

Many pitching errors can be detected by checking setup. Be sure you use the appropriate setup for the type of pitch desired. Next, check your swing motion for the desired shot.

ERROR

CORRECTION

1. Your 40-yard lob shots consistently come up short. The shot is fine from 30 yards.

2. Your basic pitch shot is hit thin or topped.

3. Your pitch and run shots are often fat.

4. Your basic pitch shot goes too far.

1. You may be hitting the wrong shot from that distance. Practice Drills 2, 3, and 4 to determine your maximum distance.

2. Check the ball position; it may be too far forward in your stance. Practice Drill 1. [Also review the Tee-Down Drills (1 and 2) on page 71 of *Golf*.]

3. Your arms may be slowing down through impact. Hold your follow-through to be sure the swing is completed. Maintain your posture through the shot.

4. Note how far past the green the shot goes. Practice Drills 2, 3, and 4, noting swing length and swing pace for each shot. Use the PW and SW. If shot continues to go too far, use the pitch and run.

Variations in Pitch Shots 57

ERROR 🚫   CORRECTION

5. Your lob shot slices too much.	5. Check your alignment and ball position. Alignment may be square rather than slightly open, and the ball position may be too far back in your stance.

Pitching Drills

1. Trajectory Control Drill

Depending on the terrain in front of the green, as well as on the green, shots of various trajectories are needed for pitching. This drill is designed to help you develop awareness of how to control the trajectory of your pitch shots. It will also help you visualize differences in ball flight, so that you will be able to imagine your shots before you hit them.

Use your sand wedge and pitching wedge and alter the ball position in your stance. Hit shots from three ball positions: center, back of center, and forward of center. Maintain your normal swing pace and three-quarter swing length. Place an alignment club on the ground toward the desired target.

Success Goal = 18 total swings from the 3 ball positions, noting differences in trajectory and visualizing the results, using your normal swing length and swing pace

  a. 9 swings with a sand wedge

    3 with a center ball position

    3 with a back-of-center ball position

    3 with a forward-of-center ball position

  b. 9 swings with a pitching wedge

    3 with a center ball position

    3 with a back-of-center ball position

    3 with a forward-of-center ball position

Your Score =

  a. Sand wedge

    (#) _____ swings, center ball position

    (#) _____ swings, back-of-center ball position

    (#) _____ swings, forward-of-center ball position

b. Pitching wedge

(#) ＿ swings, center ball position

(#) ＿ swings, back-of-center ball position

(#) ＿ swings, forward-of-center ball position

2. Basic Pitch for Distance Control (PW)

This drill incorporates the pitch shot motion and the distance control drills from Step 3. This drill and the next will help you begin to gauge your distances with the pitching wedge (PW) and sand wedge (SW).

Place seven targets in your practice area at 10-yard intervals from 30 to 90 yards. Practice the basic pitch with the PW, varying the swing length and swing pace. Note distances and trajectories as you change swing length and pace.

Success Goal = 34 total swings

a. 3-to-3 swing length, PW

5 swings, normal pace

5 swings, 1/2 pace

3 swings, normal pace

3 swings, 1/2 pace

1 swing, normal pace

b. 4-to-4 swing length, PW

5 swings, normal pace

5 swings, 1/2 pace

3 swings, normal pace

3 swings, 1/2 pace

1 swing, normal pace

Your Score = Distance hit

a. 3-to-3 swing length, PW

Shot	Pace				
	Normal	1/2	Normal	1/2	Normal
1	＿	＿	＿	＿	＿
2	＿	＿	＿	＿	
3	＿	＿	＿	＿	
4	＿	＿			
5	＿	＿			

b. 4-to-4 swing length, PW

Shot	Pace			
	Normal	1/2	Normal	1/2	Normal
1	＿	＿	＿	＿	＿
2	＿	＿	＿	＿	
3	＿	＿	＿	＿	
4	＿	＿			
5	＿	＿			

3. Basic Pitch for Distance Control (SW)

Repeat Drill 2 using your sand wedge. Compare with your distances with the PW. The SW will go a shorter distance with a higher trajectory.

Success Goal = 34 total shots

a. 3-to-3 swing length, SW

    5 swings, normal pace

    5 swings, 1/2 pace

    3 swings, normal pace

    3 swings, 1/2 pace

    1 swing, normal pace

b. 4-to-4 swing length, SW

    5 swings, normal pace

    5 swings, 1/2 pace

    3 swings, normal pace

    3 swings, 1/2 pace

    1 swing, normal pace

c. Compare your distances hit with the PW (Drill 2) and SW (Drill 3)

Your Score = Distance hit

a. 3-to-3 swing length, SW

Shot			Pace		
	Normal	1/2	Normal	1/2	Normal
1	___	___	___	___	___
2	___	___	___	___	
3	___	___	___	___	
4	___	___			
5	___	___			

b. 4-to-4 swing length, SW

Shot			Pace		
	Normal	1/2	Normal	1/2	Normal
1	___	___	___	___	___
2	___	___	___	___	
3	___	___	___	___	
4	___	___			
5	___	___			

c. Compare the distances hit with the PW versus the SW; indicate with a checkmark which goes farther

Swing length	Normal pace		1/2 Pace	
	PW	SW	PW	SW
3-to-3	___	___	___	___
4-to-4	___	___	___	___

4. Lob Pitch Distance Control

Repeat Drill 2 using the lob pitch shot. Select a sand wedge, which is specifically designed to create a higher, softer shot and produce less roll and therefore less distance. Remember, the lob pitch uses a 4-to-4 swing length. Review setup and swing motion to note the differences from the basic pitch.

Success Goal = 21 total swings

5 swings, normal pace

5 swings, 1/2 pace

3 swings, normal pace

5 swings, 1/2 pace

3 swings, normal pace

Your Score = Distance hit

Shot	Pace				
	Normal	1/2	Normal	1/2	Normal
1	___	___	___	___	___
2	___	___	___	___	___
3	___	___	___	___	___
4	___	___		___	
5	___	___		___	

5. Pitch and Run Trajectory Control

Place seven targets in your practice area at 10-yard intervals, beginning at 10 yards. This drill will help you to learn to predict your landing area (not the amount of roll) as you practice visualizing shots that you need to carry over or land short of the targets. Say, for example, you're 10 yards from a green with a high apron. You need to carry the ball safely onto the green. If the ball lands short of the green in the high grass, it will stop.

Put yourself into game situations or compete with a friend. Using a PW, start at 10 yards and work up to the longer distances. Select and check your goal—short, long, or on target. Then hit the shot and indicate if the goal was met. Vary the distances and alter your club selection. Practice with the 6-iron through the SW. (Note: This drill can be done in one or several sessions.)

Success Goal = 66 total shots, 22 each with a PW, SW, and choice of club

2 shots, 10 yards

2 shots, 20 yards

2 shots, 30 yards

2 shots, 40 yards

2 shots, 50 yards

2 shots, 60 yards

2 shots, 70 yards

1 shot, 40 yards

1 shot, 10 yards

1 shot, 30 yards

1 shot, 50 yards

1 shot, 20 yards

1 shot, 60 yards

1 shot, 10 yards

1 shot, 70 yards

Your Score = 75 percent of shots successfully meeting selected yardage goal

Shots	Yards	Short			On target			Long			Goal met		
		PW	SW	Club	PW	SW	Club	PW	SW	Club	PW	SW	Club
Example:													
a	20	✔	___	___	___	✔	___	___	___	6-i	*no*	*yes*	*no*
b	20	___	___	___	✔	✔	6-i	___	___	___	*yes*	*yes*	*yes*
1	10	___	___	___	___	___	___	___	___	___	___	___	___
2	10	___	___	___	___	___	___	___	___	___	___	___	___
3	20	___	___	___	___	___	___	___	___	___	___	___	___
4	20	___	___	___	___	___	___	___	___	___	___	___	___
5	30	___	___	___	___	___	___	___	___	___	___	___	___
6	30	___	___	___	___	___	___	___	___	___	___	___	___
7	40	___	___	___	___	___	___	___	___	___	___	___	___
8	40	___	___	___	___	___	___	___	___	___	___	___	___
9	50	___	___	___	___	___	___	___	___	___	___	___	___
10	50	___	___	___	___	___	___	___	___	___	___	___	___
11	60	___	___	___	___	___	___	___	___	___	___	___	___
12	60	___	___	___	___	___	___	___	___	___	___	___	___
13	70	___	___	___	___	___	___	___	___	___	___	___	___
14	70	___	___	___	___	___	___	___	___	___	___	___	___
15	10	___	___	___	___	___	___	___	___	___	___	___	___
16	40	___	___	___	___	___	___	___	___	___	___	___	___
17	30	___	___	___	___	___	___	___	___	___	___	___	___
18	50	___	___	___	___	___	___	___	___	___	___	___	___
19	20	___	___	___	___	___	___	___	___	___	___	___	___
20	70	___	___	___	___	___	___	___	___	___	___	___	___
21	30	___	___	___	___	___	___	___	___	___	___	___	___
22	60	___	___	___	___	___	___	___	___	___	___	___	___
Total		___	___	___	___	___	___	___	___	___	___	___	___
Percentage											___	___	___

6. On-Course Pitching Situations Drill

The pitch shot has the greatest variability in distance and shot options. Your individual preference and ability to execute the options, given the lie of the ball, determine your shot choice. Go with your strengths on the course and in considering the following situations.

Situation A:

You are 30 yards from the green. There is a bunker between your ball and the green. The green is elevated, and pin placement is 60 feet from the near edge of the green.

Success Goal = Answer the following questions for Situation A

1. What are your shot options?
2. What is the best option and club selection?

Your Score = Answers to the questions

1. Shot options:

   a. _____

   b. _____

   c. _____

2. Best option and club selection: _____

Situation B:

Your ball has landed 15 yards from the green. There are no hazards between your ball and the green, and the pin is 10 yards from the near edge of the green.

Success Goal = Answer the following questions for Situation B

1. What are your shot options?
2. What is the best option and club selection?

Your Score = Answers to the questions

1. Shot options:

   a. _____

   b. _____

   c. _____

2. Best option and club selection: _____

Situation C:

Your ball has landed 10 yards from the green. The green is elevated, and there is a trap between your ball and the pin. The pin is 15 feet from the near fringe.

Success Goal = Answer the following questions for Situation C

1. What are your shot options?
2. What is the best option and club selection?

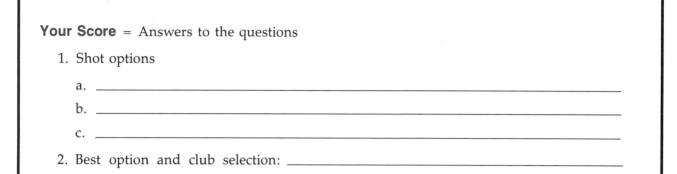

Your Score = Answers to the questions

1. Shot options

   a. _____

   b. _____

   c. _____

2. Best option and club selection: _____

Pitching
Keys to Success Checklists

The pitch shot is important to improving your ability to score. Because of the wide range of distances for which the pitch is used, specific practice in distance control is a must.

Setup positions for the lob and the pitch and run shot are the key elements. They vary slightly from your basic pitch shot setup.

Because the pitch shot is the most fundamental approach shot from areas near the green, consistency is critical. Being able to selectively use the lob, basic pitch, and pitch and run shot will give you increased options for scoring.

Have your teacher or coach or a trained observer evaluate your progress using the checklists in Figures 4.3 and 4.5. Once you have a consistent pitch shot, you will be on your way to better golf.

Answers to Drill 6

Situation A

1. Shot options:

   a. Basic pitch shot—allows high trajectory with minimal roll
   b. Lob—this distance is too far for good distance control
   c. Pitch and run—risky control because of the trap
2. Basic pitch shot with PW or SW, depending on distance ability

Situation B

1. Shot options:
   a. Pitch and run—allows for minimal trajectory and roll control
   b. Lob—high trajectory *not* needed; in the 10 yards, can roll the ball to pin
   c. Basic pitch—high trajectory *not* needed
2. Pitch and run with PW is preferred

Situation C

1. Shot options
   a. Lob—creates high trajectory with little to no roll, which is needed due to the short distance and little green between the fringe and pin
   b. Basic pitch—distance too short to have much control in getting the ball close with a basic pitch; swing pace would need to be too slow
   c. Pitch and run—the bunker and the short distance from the fringe to the pin makes this a difficult shot to get close to the pin
2. Lob with SW or lofted wedge

Step 5 Chip Shot Variation

You will see the biggest improvement in your game when you spend time practicing the short game. Chipping and putting are two areas in which strength is not a factor. You may not find these shots as exciting as hitting the long shots, but the rewards may be greater in terms of lowering your score.

You will now be learning another type of chip shot—"off-green putting." That might seem a confusing name for a chip shot, but that's what golf teachers call it! The off-green putting shot combines, as you may infer from the name, elements of basic chipping and putting techniques. It is used from a short distance off the green when ground conditions prohibit using your regular putting stroke. This is the next most accurate stroke to putting.

WHY IS OFF-GREEN PUTTING IMPORTANT?

The key to scoring around the green is to get the ball as close as you can to the hole—or sink it if you can. You may have already experienced the thrill of holing a chip shot or getting your chips close enough to one-putt. That saves a lot of shots. Off-green putting is another stroke saver.

Off-green putting is not a replacement for the basic chip shot. It has two limitations. It requires a good lie, and it is not as effective as the chip shot at distances greater than 60 or 70 feet. With practice you will find your maximum effective distance. The basic chip can be used in good and bad lie situations and has greater distance capability. When your lie is good and the distance is within the range of either shot, go with the off-green putting technique if you feel comfortable with it. It is a higher percentage shot.

HOW TO EXECUTE OFF-GREEN PUTTING

The off-green putting stroke combines your putting and chipping techniques. If you are using the target-hand low putting stroke illustrated in Step 7, you will need to adapt one of the other two styles for this shot. Note the setup positions for the three strokes (putting, chipping, and off-green putting) in Figure 5.1, a-c. This will help you prepare visually to see how the chip and putt techniques blend to become off-green putting.

The putting stroke is the most accurate stroke in golf. You are closer to the ball, and your eyes are directly over the target line. This combination allows the club to stay on path to the target more effectively. In off-green putting, you adapt your putting stroke to the use of an iron.

The basic chip shot is a low-trajectory shot that minimizes or eliminates the use of the wrists, as does the putt. This increases accuracy and provides better distance control. In the setup, as illustrated in Figure 5.1c, ball position is just back of center, with the upper body leaning toward the target. The setup creates the low

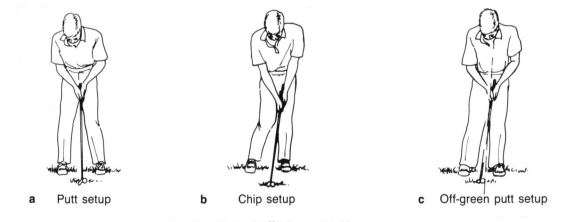

a   Putt setup   b   Chip setup   c   Off-green putt setup

Figure 5.1 A comparison of putt (a), chip (b), and off-green putt (c) setups.

trajectory, allowing the club to contact the ball with a slightly descending angle. This provides more control and gives the ball its trajectory.

Select a 6-iron to learn the stroke. Take your putter out, and set your 6-iron to the same lie (see Figure 5.2, a and b); the shafts of the clubs should be parallel. Note that the head of the 6-iron is not sitting flat on the ground—it is tilted on the toe. With practice you will adjust to this.

a   6-iron   **b**

Figure 5.2 Setting your 6-iron to the lie of your putter.

Keeping the 6-iron in the same lie as your putter, take your putting grip, stance, and posture. The club is longer, so be sure to grip down on the grip so club length is the same as with your putter. Your eyes should be positioned directly over the target line as shown in Figure 5.3.

Figure 5.3 Off-green putting setup with eyes over the target line.

Position the ball just back of center in your stance, and lean toward the target side (see Figure 5.4, a and b). This is your chip setup position. Note that this positions your hands, your head, and the buttons of your shirt, or your sternum, to the target side of the ball.

Swing motion is the same as in your putting stroke, and backswing and forwardswing are equal in length. There is no wrist motion; your hands and arms work as a unit. This pendular motion is illustrated in the Keys to Success shown in Figure 5.5. Note the follow-through. Your hands and arms are in the same position as the address position. Hold this position at the end of your stroke. If the clubhead has passed your hands, your wrists have been active. This adds undesired loft to the shot and reduces distance and accuracy control. The off-green putting stroke will be longer than the putting stroke for the same distance, because of the loft. You will adjust to this easily as you practice.

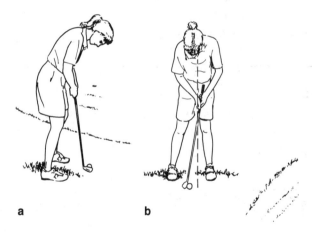

a   **b**

Figure 5.4 Setup for off-green putting.

Figure 5.5 Keys to Success:
  Off-Green Putting

**Preparation
Phase**

Pre-Setup

1. Read the green ____
2. Select the intermediate target ____
3. Select the club ____

Setup

1. Grip in palms ____
2. Shoulders square ____
3. Hips square ____
4. Feet square ____
5. Feet shoulder-width apart ____
6. Weight toward target side ____
7. Weight instep to balls of feet ____
8. Arms hanging freely
9. Eyes over target line ____
10. Center ball position ____
11. Blade square ____
12. Head and swing center target side of ball ____
13. Hands positioned off inside of target leg ____

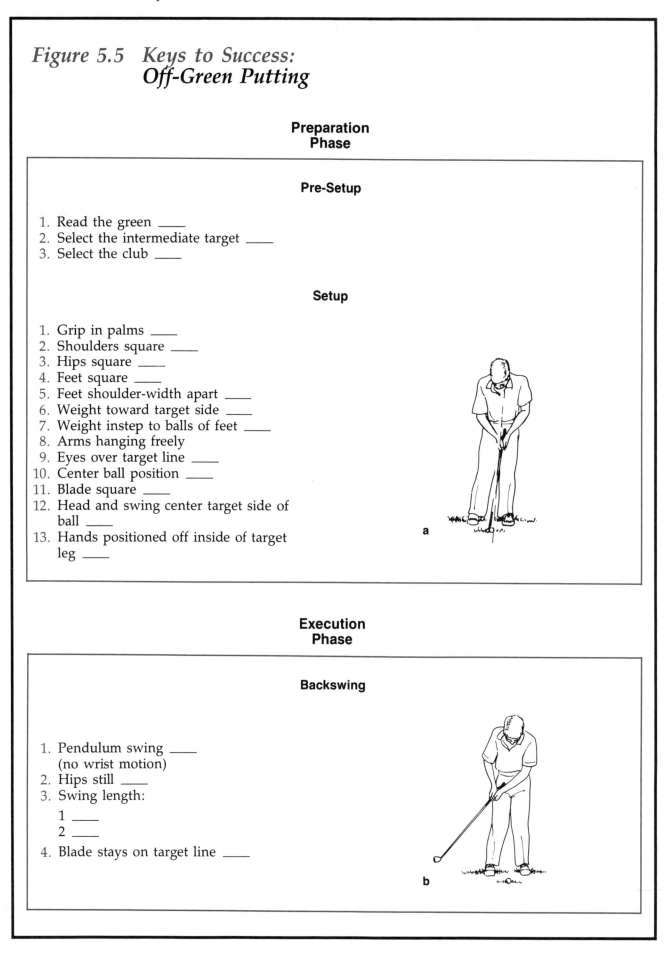

a

**Execution
Phase**

Backswing

1. Pendulum swing ____
   (no wrist motion)
2. Hips still ____
3. Swing length:

   1 ____

   2 ____

4. Blade stays on target line ____

b

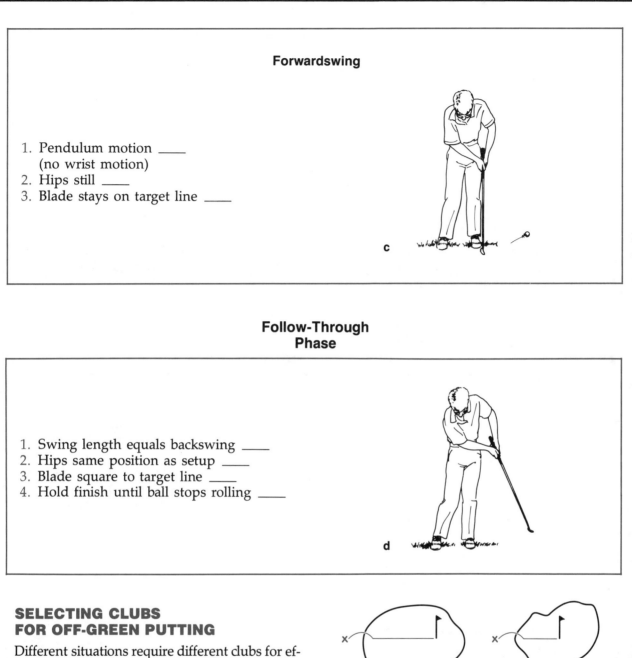

Forwardswing

1. Pendulum motion ____
   (no wrist motion)
2. Hips still ____
3. Blade stays on target line ____

c

**Follow-Through
Phase**

1. Swing length equals backswing ____
2. Hips same position as setup ____
3. Blade square to target line ____
4. Hold finish until ball stops rolling ____

d

SELECTING CLUBS
FOR OFF-GREEN PUTTING

Different situations require different clubs for effective results. Figure 5.6, a-c, shows three distances across the green to the pin. Any club could be used for the off-green putting stroke. However, you may find it easiest to use a three-club system: 6, 8, and PW. The 6-iron has the least loft and provides more roll with a shorter stroke. The 8-iron provides more loft than the 6-iron and less roll. The PW provides the greatest loft and least roll. The 6-iron would be recommended for the longer distances (see Figure 5.6a), the 8-iron for the medium distances (see Figure 5.6b), and the PW for the short distances (see Figure 5.6c). With practice you will be able to select the most effective club for your stroke.

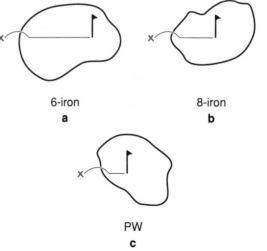

6-iron
a

8-iron
b

PW
c

Figure 5.6 Club selection based on distance to the flag.

The off-green putting stroke is most effective close to the green. Remember that the stroke is a putting stroke with a combined chip and putting setup. When the stroke length exceeds the length of your putting stroke, then it is no longer effective, and the basic chip should be used. To determine the maximum distance for your off-green putting shot, begin hitting balls, moving back from the green to the distance at which the shot is forced. Then move in 4 or 5 feet, noting this distance as your maximum for control.

Detecting Off-Green Putting Errors

Off-green putting errors can be readily detected because of the stroke's compactness. Remember, it combines elements of both the putting and the chipping techniques. You are seeking a shot trajectory that has minimum air time and maximum roll.

ERROR 🚫

CORRECTION

1. The ball goes too high and short.

1a. Check your setup. Ball position may be too far forward. Or you may not have enough body lean toward the target.
1b. Hold your finish. Be sure your wrists are not active, causing a flipping motion. Check the swing length. Forwardswing should equal backswing.

2. The ball is topped and rolls too far.

2a. Ball position may be too far back in your stance and you may be moving laterally on your forwardswing.
2b. You may be moving your upper body on the forwardswing. Practice the pendulum swing, using a mirror to check it.

ERROR ⊘	CORRECTION
3. The ball goes high and too far.	3. Check your finish. Your hands may be too active and your swing too long. Compare your finish to Error 1.
4. Swing technique is good, but distance control is inconsistent.	4. Practice Distance Drill 3, alternating a 6- and an 8-iron. Note the corresponding distances with changes in swing length and swing pace.
5. Contact and distance are good, but direction is inconsistent.	5. Check alignment and setup first. Practice Track Drill 2.

Chip Shot Drills

1. Mirror Drill for Setup

Off-green putting combines the putt setup and the chip shot lean with the swing center more toward the target side. Refer to the setup position for off-green putting in Figure 5.1b. This position is initially awkward, but with practice it becomes more comfortable. First practice taking your setup position in front of a mirror. Then practice taking your setup position and making the stroke, using a mirror. This will help you to identify the feel with the way it looks. Be sure to match your iron to the more upright lie of the putter.

Success Goal = 10 setups using a 6-iron, and 10 setups and strokes using a 6-iron, all in front of a mirror

Your Score =

a. (#) _____ setups
b. (#) _____ setups and strokes

2. Track Drill

This drill will help you feel the path of the off-green putting stroke. Place two clubs on the ground parallel to the target line and just farther apart than your iron blade. Practice swinging between the clubs, using a pendular motion and keeping the blade square as it moves back and forth.

Success Goal = 15 strokes without hitting either of the parallel clubs, using a 6-iron

Your Score = (#) _____ strokes

3. Distance Drill

Practice your stroke, checking for the square blade at finish and noting the distance the ball goes with each swing.

Place five clubs in a ladder formation. The first club should be 10 feet from the fringe of the green, with the other clubs at 3-foot intervals (10, 13, 16, 19, and 22 feet). Practice chipping for distance; don't worry about aiming at a target or hole. For example, decide to chip the distance between the second and third clubs of the ladder. Place your balls about 3 or 4 feet off the fringe of the green.

Success Goal = Use your off-green putting stroke to chip 15 total balls with an 8-iron, attempting to make the balls quit rolling between the desired club distances

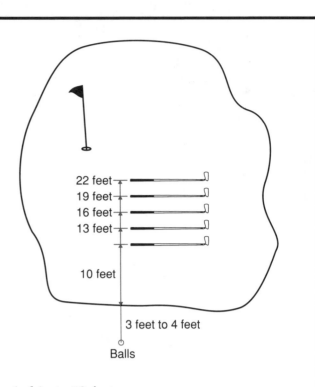

2 chips to 10 feet

2 chips to 13 feet

2 chips to 16 feet

2 chips to 19 feet

2 chips to 22 feet

1 chip to 13 feet

1 chip to 22 feet

1 chip to 10 feet

1 chip to 19 feet

1 chip to 16 feet

Your Score =

(#) ____ chips to 10 feet

(#) ____ chips to 13 feet

(#) ____ chips to 16 feet

(#) ____ chips to 19 feet

(#) ____ chips to 22 feet

(#) ____ chip to 13 feet

(#) ____ chip to 22 feet

(#) ____ chip to 10 feet

(#) ____ chip to 19 feet

(#) ____ chip to 16 feet

4. Alternate Club Distance Drill

Repeat Drill 3, alternating between the 6-iron, 8-iron, and PW. Note the differences in roll and trajectory of the balls hit with different clubs. By experimenting with different clubs, you may find you are more effective with a particular club and not others, *or* you may find more versatility with all three. This drill will help you determine your distance control at varying distances.

Success Goal = 15 total chips alternating between the 6-iron, 8-iron, and PW

3 chips to 10 feet (6, 8, PW)

3 chips to 19 feet (6, 8, PW)

3 chips to 13 feet (6, 8, PW)

3 chips to 22 feet (6, 8, PW)

3 chips to 16 feet (6, 8, PW)

Your Score =

(#) ____ chips to 10 feet (6)

(#) ____ chips to 10 feet (8)

(#) ____ chips to 10 feet (PW)

(#) ____ chips to 19 feet (6)

(#) ____ chips to 19 feet (8)

(#) ____ chips to 19 feet (PW)

(#) ____ chips to 13 feet (6)

(#) ____ chips to 13 feet (8)

(#) ____ chips to 13 feet (PW)

(#) ____ chips to 22 feet (6)

(#) ____ chips to 22 feet (8)

(#) ____ chips to 22 feet (PW)

(#) ____ chips to 16 feet (6)

(#) ____ chips to 16 feet (8)

(#) ____ chips to 16 feet (PW)

5. Cluster Drill

This drill will help you develop a repeating stroke. Place three balls about 5 feet off the green in a line, 5 inches apart. Without watching its roll, chip the first ball. Still without watching the rolls, chip the next two balls, trying to have the balls come to rest in a cluster, nudging each other. Focus on the feel of the stroke. Practice with the 6-iron, 8-iron, and PW.

Success Goal = 15 total chips using an 8-iron, focusing on developing a feel for the repeated stroke and hitting the first ball in each group of 3 to a new location. Repeat this drill with a 6-iron and a PW.

3 chips to location A (1st ball)

3 chips to location B (4th ball)

3 chips to location C (7th ball)

3 chips to location D (10th ball)

3 chips to location E (13th ball)

Your Score =

(#) ____ chips to location A

(#) ____ chips to location B

(#) ____ chips to location C

(#) ____ chips to location D

(#) ____ chips to location E

6. Off-Green Line Drill

The off-green putting technique has a distance limitation. This drill will help you find out how far off the green you can use the stroke without forcing it and help you learn to predict the trajectory needed to land on the green.

Select a target (hole) about 21 feet from the fringe of a green and place five balls 12 to 16 inches apart, in a line away from the hole. Practice chipping, starting with the ball closest to the green. Practice with the 6-iron, 8-iron, and PW. When you can no longer land the ball on the green without forcing the shot, you have exceeded your control distance. Go back to your last distance of safely landing on the green. This becomes your maximum distance to use the off-green putting shot with a particular club. Beyond this distance you need to use your basic chip shot.

Success Goal = 15 total chips, focusing on the feel for distance and trajectory

    5 chips with a 6-iron

    5 chips with an 8-iron

    5 chips with a PW

Your Score =

    (#) ____ chips with a 6-iron

    (#) ____ chips with an 8-iron

    (#) ____ chips with a PW

7. On-Course Off-Green Putting Drills

Shots around the green are control shots, for which feel and finesse are as important as good technique. The general rule of thumb when immediately adjacent to a green is, "If you can putt, putt." When putting is not an option, the next shots in order of accuracy are off-green putting and basic chipping. It is important, when playing a round of golf, that you go with your strengths.

In the following situations, provide all options and club selections, and indicate your current preference.

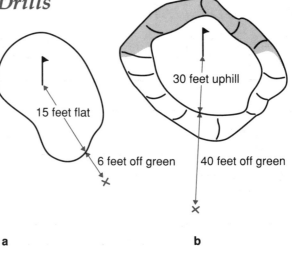

a   b

Situation A:

Your ball is 6 feet off the green with a good lie. The pin is 15 feet from the near fringe. The terrain is flat.

Success Goal = Respond to the following questions for Situation A

    1. What are your shot options? What are the advantages and disadvantages of each?

    2. What club would you use for each option?

    3. Indicate your preferred option.

Your Score = Answers to the questions

1.   **Shot options**   **Advantages**   **Disadvantages**

      a. _____   _____   _____

      b. _____   _____   _____

      c. _____   _____   _____

2. Club selections to match options:

    a. _____

    b. _____

    c. _____

3. Preferred option: _____

Situation B:

   The ball is resting in a divot 40 feet off the green. The pin is 30 feet from the fringe on an uphill slope.

Success Goal = Respond to the following questions for Situation B

   1. What are your shot options?

   2. What club would you select for each option?

   3. Indicate your preferred option.

Your Score = Answers to the questions

1.

Shot options	Advantages	Disadvantages
a. _____	_____	_____
b. _____	_____	_____

2. Club selections to match options:

    a. _____

    b. _____

3. Preferred option: _____

Off-Green Putting
Keys to Success Checklist

Your off-green putting combines the chipping and putting stroke setups. As an advanced golfer, you need to know not only how to execute the skills, but also when to choose which skill. Have your teacher or coach or a trained observer evaluate your stroke qualitatively, using the checklist in Figure 5.5, and also give you feedback about the appropriateness of your shot selection.

Answers to Drill 7

Situation A:

1. *Shot options*	*Advantages*	*Disadvantages*
a. Putt	Control	It is difficult to control pace on a putt with 6 feet of long grass before the green
b. Off-green putting	Control, focus on distance, and feel, without concern of ball hitting into longer grass	(None)
c. Basic chip	Control	Farther away from ball, not as accurate as putt or off-green putting for distance or accuracy

2. *Club selection*
   a. Putt—putter
   b. Off-green putting—6-iron, or 8-iron
   c. Basic chip—8-iron, or PW

3. Select the club in which you have the most confidence.

Situation B:

1. *Shot options*	*Advantages*	*Disadvantages*
a. Basic chip	Control distance and direction from poor lie	(None)
b. Pitch and run	Control if not strong enough for basic chip	Harder to control distance

2. *Club Selection*		
a. PW, SW	Loft provides greater security from a poor lie	(None)
b. PW, SW	Loft provides greater security from a poor lie	(None)

3. Selected club: PW for a Basic Chip Shot

Step 6 Sand Shot Considerations

Sand shots generally comprise a very small percentage of shots in a round of golf, depending on the number of traps and on your state of mind. When your game is off or you're worrying about the sand, you may feel in danger of hitting into every trap on the course, just because of your heightened anxiety. On other days, you might not be aware of the sand at all.

Our first goal, now, is to reduce your sand anxiety by helping to explain some of the differences between your good sand days and those you want to forget. Our second goal is to teach you the techniques for producing high and low trap shots and keys for hitting fairway bunker shots.

WHY ARE SAND SHOT CONSIDERATIONS IMPORTANT?

Technique is not always the cause of poor sand play. Think about the sand shots you've played recently. Was the sand white, or dark like dirt, or light orange? Was it soft and powdery or heavy and coarse? When you stepped in the trap, did your feet sink, or was the sand firm? Was the sand dry or wet? Did it change from one course to the next? Or one trap to the next? How high was the lip (edge) of the trap? Did your sand play vary?

You may not have noticed anything about the sand other than the fact that the ball was in the sand. This is not uncommon. However, to be consistent in sand play, you need to raise your awareness in order to evaluate your sand shot effectively. Your goals change from "getting out and on" to "getting close" (to the pin). The type of sand wedge you select, sand texture, trap design, and shot trajectory are all considerations in making consistent sand shots to lower your score.

HOW TO APPLY SAND SHOT CONSIDERATIONS

Players who execute good sand shots have spent hours in the sand, learning to enjoy its challenges. In time the sand will become your "friend"—after all, it's the only shot in golf that you can hit "fat" and be rewarded!

To understand and execute effective sand shots, you must understand that the sand wedge is a special type of club, used in many different situations. You must also understand the differing characteristics of various types of sand.

Equipment

Sand wedges are designed specifically for use in the sand. But they also are effective for various types of shots outside the trap. Not all sand wedges have the same design. There are reasons for this: Players' needs vary with their abilities, and the texture of sand varies from very fine and powdery to heavy and coarse like dirt.

Let's look at the design of the sand wedges and pitching wedge in Figure 6.1. Note the soles of the clubs. The lead edge is the front portion of the club, and the trail edge the back. You may hear the sole referred to as the "flange" or "bounce" of the club. Irons (2 through PW) are designed to contact the ground and clip the grass, taking a divot. This is possible because the lead edge is higher than the trailing edge and allows the club to "dig" slightly as it contacts the ground (see Figure 6.1a). The lead edge is often termed the "digger." "Digging" is not effective or desired in the sand unless the ball is buried, and then adjustments are made.

The designs of the sand wedges in Figure 6.1, b and c, are noticeably different. On wedge c, the trail edge is higher than the lead edge, and the width of the flange tends to be wider. This design allows the club to literally "bounce" off the sand rather than dig in. This creates a shallow displacement of sand as opposed to the steeper displacement created by a pitching wedge. Remember, in a sand shot, the ball rides out with the sand. A shallow displacement allows more clubhead momentum to continue forward to get the ball out of the trap, whereas a steeper displacement tends to decelerate, and often stop, clubhead momentum, causing missed shots.

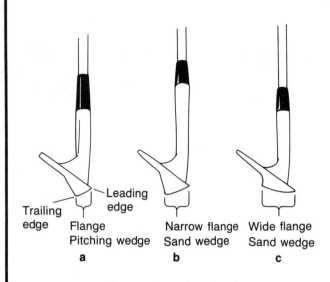

Figure 6.1 Pitching and sand wedge flanges.

Sand Texture and the Appropriate Sand Wedge

Most courses will have the same type of sand in all the traps. However, the depth of the sand may vary due to drainage, trap design, and weather. You can select a sand wedge suitable for the traps you most commonly encounter. For example, if you play on courses with light, fluffy, or powdery sand, you need a sand wedge with a wide flange with the lead edge lower than the trail edge (as shown in Figure 6.1c). This design allows the club to skid or bounce through the sand rather than to dig.

In contrast, firm, coarse sand is best played with a sand wedge that has a thinner flange and less height difference between the lead and trail edges (as shown in Figure 6.1b). Less bounce is desired in firm sand, because there is less sand under the ball to cushion the club. In firm sand, a club with too much bounce will tend to contact the ball, resulting in thin shots.

If you play courses that have different types of sand, you may want to consider carrying two sand wedges. Ask the professional what type of sand the course has, then declare the extra wedge out of play. This means it cannot be used during the round. If you are playing in a tournament, be sure to remove it from your bag.

CONTROLLING TRAJECTORY IN GREENSIDE BUNKERS

Greenside traps vary in design. Some are deep with high lips, and others are shallow and level with the green. If you have a good lie (i.e., not

buried) in the sand, when the trap is deep, you want a high trajectory. When the trap is shallow and has a low lip, you have the option of either a high or a low trajectory. The higher trajectory tends to roll less than the lower trajectory.

Imagine a teacup and saucer. The sides of the teacup are steeper than the sides of the saucer (see Figure 6.2, a and b). The saucer is shallow. The high-trajectory shot is hit with a more vertical angle of club approach, as if swinging up the side of the teacup. The lower trajectory shot is produced with a shallower swing motion, more like your regular full swing, as if swinging along the surface of the saucer.

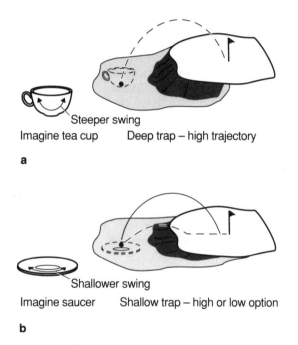

Figure 6.2 Greenside bunker designs.

High Trajectory

The high-trajectory shot is the "explosion shot." To set up for the high-trajectory shot, keep your shoulders, hips, and feet slightly open (see left column, Figure 6.3a). Dig your feet into the sand, with the balls of your feet lower than the heels. This will help you maintain your posture. The ball is positioned forward of center in your stance, and your clubface is open. Be sure to open the clubface first, then grip it.

The open position makes your swing motion more vertical. Make your regular swing (see left column, Figure 6.3b). You should feel as though the club is bouncing off the sand. The open clubface allows more of the trailing edge to contact the sand to prevent digging.

The forwardswing motion (see left column, Figure 6.3c) feels as though your rear hand is under your target hand, or as if your rear hand palm is facing up, as the club swings through the sand. The wrists do not recock in this shot during your follow-through (see left column, Figure 6.3d).

If you tend to hit too far behind the ball using an even weight distribution, set your weight more forward of center. This will alter your club entry to the sand.

You may have trouble hitting longer trap shots with the open position. Squaring your stance and the clubface will help, and recocking your wrists will provide additional clubhead acceleration for longer shots. Then practice modifying the ball position to find your distance. Remember, the more forward the ball is positioned, the more sand and less distance.

Low Trajectory

Low-trajectory shots are hit from buried lies or good lies. Low-trajectory shots are played similarly to a pitch and run shot. The setup position for the low-trajectory shot is illustrated in Figure 6.3a (right column). Shoulders are square, hips and feet are slightly open. The feet are dug in as in the high-trajectory shot. Weight is more toward the target side, with the ball positioned center to slightly back of center. The clubface is square rather than open.

The swing motion length is between 3 and 4, depending upon the distance. The key is to continue your swing motion through the ball (see right column, Figure 6.3, b-d). There is a great tendency to stop on this shot. Remember, the sand is a buffer, reducing the distance, so the ball won't go as far as the same pitch and run from grass.

Figure 6.3   Keys to Success: Controlling Sand Shot Trajectory

(*indicates variation from full swing)

Preparation Phase

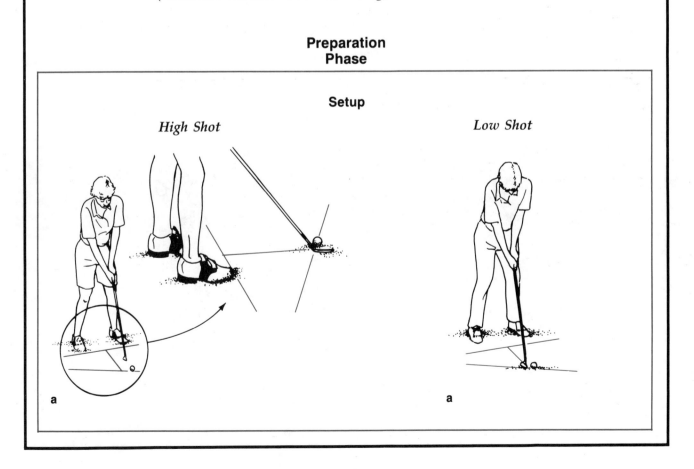

Setup

High Shot

Low Shot

a

a

		High Shot		Low Shot	

High Shot   _Low Shot_

_____ 1. Neutral grip position _____

_____ 2. Feet shoulder-width apart _____

3. Weight even _____   *3. Weight more toward target side _____

_____ 4. Weight instep to balls of the feet _____

*_____ 5. Toes dug into sand *_____

*_____ 6. Alignment:

*_____   a. Feet open *_____

*_____   b. Hips open *_____

*c. Shoulders open _____   c. Shoulders square _____

_____ 7. Posture with flat back _____

*8. Ball position: 2 to 3 inches target side of center _____   *8. Ball position: Center to rear side _____

*9. Blade open _____   *9. Blade square to delofted _____

Execution Phase

Backswing

High Shot   _Low Shot_

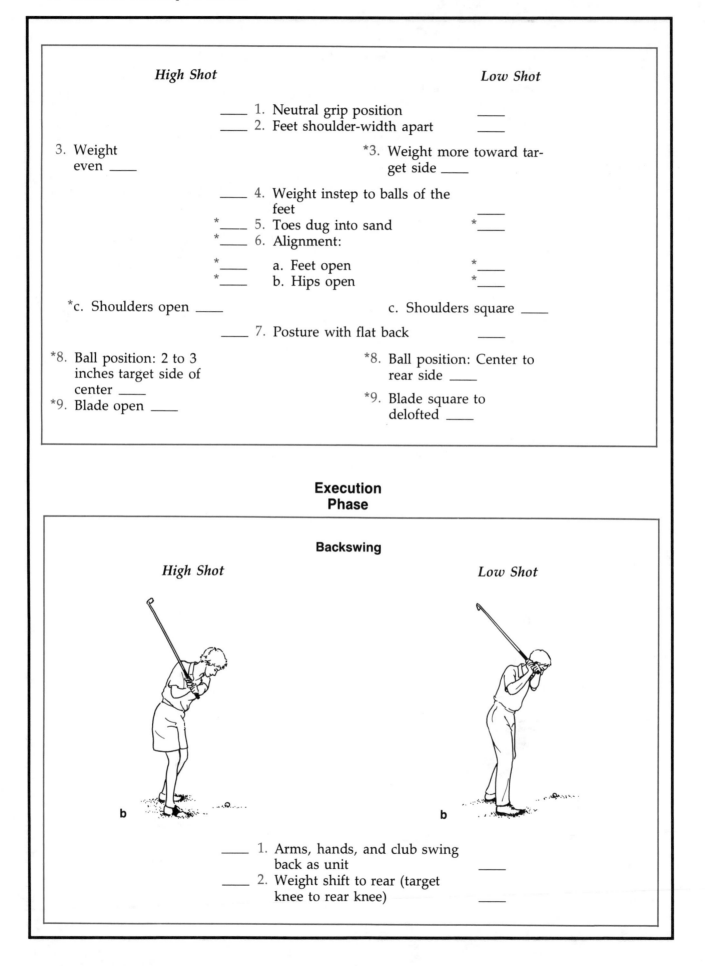

b   b

_____ 1. Arms, hands, and club swing back as unit _____

_____ 2. Weight shift to rear (target knee to rear knee) _____

	High Shot		*Low Shot*

_____ 3. Wrists cocked by hip level   _____
_____ 4. Hips turned 45° to rear   _____

5. Backswing length: 5. Backswing length:
   *3 _____   *3 _____
   *4 _____   *4 _____

Forwardswing

High Shot	*Low Shot*

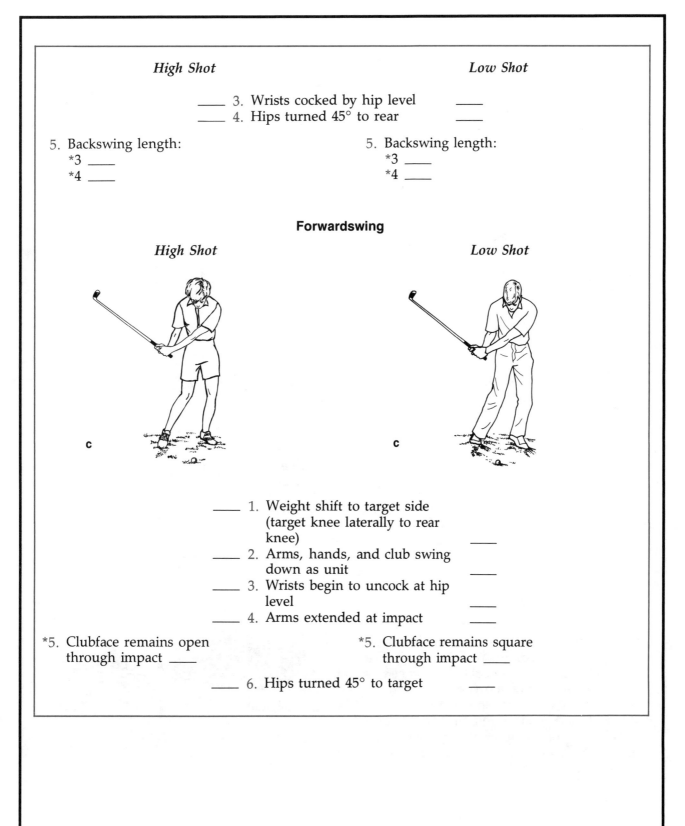

c   c

_____ 1. Weight shift to target side
       (target knee laterally to rear
       knee)   _____
_____ 2. Arms, hands, and club swing
       down as unit   _____
_____ 3. Wrists begin to uncock at hip
       level   _____
_____ 4. Arms extended at impact   _____

*5. Clubface remains open   *5. Clubface remains square
through impact _____   through impact _____

_____ 6. Hips turned 45° to target   _____

Follow-Through Phase

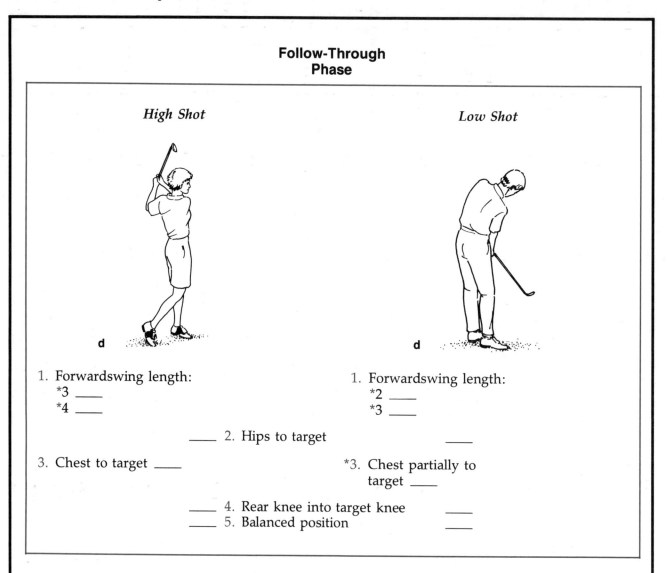

High Shot

Low Shot

1. Forwardswing length:
   *3 _____
   *4 _____

_____ 2. Hips to target

3. Chest to target _____

1. Forwardswing length:
   *2 _____
   *3 _____

_____

*3. Chest partially to
   target _____

_____ 4. Rear knee into target knee   _____
_____ 5. Balanced position   _____

FAIRWAY BUNKER SHOTS

A fairway bunker shot is played similarly to your regular fairway shot. The lie of the ball determines what you can do. You should hit a buried lie back into play without trying any heroics. You can waste a lot of unnecessary shots trying to hit a great shot from a poor lie.

If you have a good lie, your first consideration is the height of the lip on the fairway bunker and the ball's distance from it. This determines the potential club selection (see Figure 6.4). The closer the ball is to the lip, the more lofted the club selection. You need to select the club that will get the ball safely back into play. This may not always be the club needed to reach the target. If the lip is not a problem, and the lie is good, club selection is open.

The setup position for the fairway bunker shot is the same as your regular full swing, with two

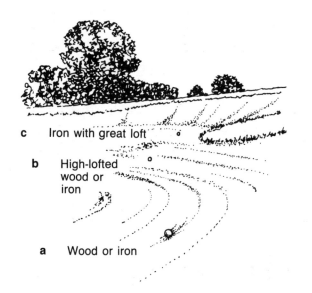

c   Iron with great loft

b   High-lofted
    wood or
    iron

a   Wood or iron

Figure 6.4 Fairway bunker club considerations based on ball distances from the lip and ball line.

modifications. Because the sand tends to reduce your stability during the swing, dig in slightly with the balls of your feet, and dig the inside of your rear foot in slightly.

The second modification is in the grip position. Because you have dug your feet in slightly, if you don't modify your grip, the club will enter the sand before reaching the ball, which is what you want in the greenside bunkers. But in the fairway bunkers, you want the club to contact the bottom of the ball. So grip down about 1 or 2 inches from your regular grip. This grip position will adjust for the feet dug into the sand, reducing the amount of club-sand contact. Hitting a thin shot from a fairway bunker is more productive than hitting a fat shot. Figure 6.5, a-d, shows keys to correct technique for your fairway bunker shots.

Figure 6.5 Keys to Success: Fairway Bunker Shots

(*indicates variation from the normal full swing)

Preparation Phase

Setup

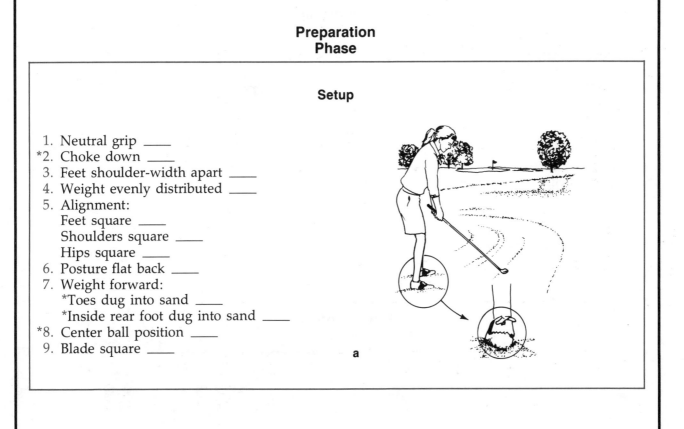

1. Neutral grip ____
*2. Choke down ____
3. Feet shoulder-width apart ____
4. Weight evenly distributed ____
5. Alignment:
   Feet square ____
   Shoulders square ____
   Hips square ____
6. Posture flat back ____
7. Weight forward:
   *Toes dug into sand ____
   *Inside rear foot dug into sand ____
*8. Center ball position ____
9. Blade square ____

a

Execution
Phase

Backswing

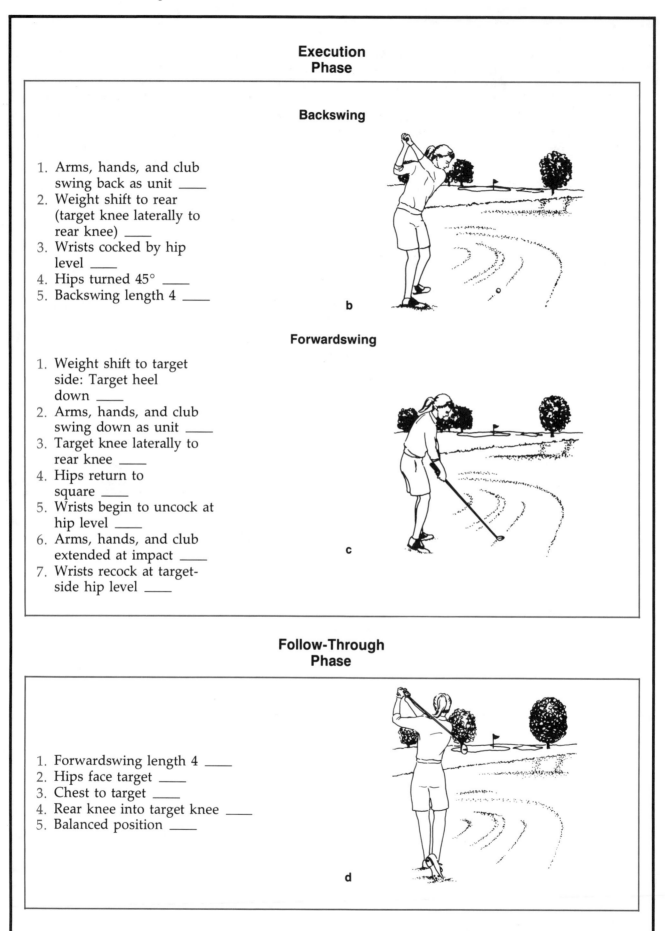

1. Arms, hands, and club swing back as unit ____
2. Weight shift to rear (target knee laterally to rear knee) ____
3. Wrists cocked by hip level ____
4. Hips turned 45° ____
5. Backswing length 4 ____

b

Forwardswing

1. Weight shift to target side: Target heel down ____
2. Arms, hands, and club swing down as unit ____
3. Target knee laterally to rear knee ____
4. Hips return to square ____
5. Wrists begin to uncock at hip level ____
6. Arms, hands, and club extended at impact ____
7. Wrists recock at target-side hip level ____

c

Follow-Through
Phase

1. Forwardswing length 4 ____
2. Hips face target ____
3. Chest to target ____
4. Rear knee into target knee ____
5. Balanced position ____

d

Detecting Errors in Sand Play

Review the considerations for effective sand play before evaluating yours. Note the sand texture, the trap design relative to the height of the lip, the lie of the ball, the desired trajectory, and the design of your sand wedge.

ERROR 🚫

CORRECTION

ERROR	CORRECTION
1. Distance is inconsistent from greenside bunkers.	1. Practice Drill 3.
2. The ball comes out consistently from greenside bunkers, but the trajectory is low.	2a. Check ball position and clubface alignment. If ball position is too far back, clubface tends to be delofted, creating a low trajectory.
	2b. Check swing length. If swing is too short (i.e., 3 or less), a low trajectory may result.
3. Shots are hit thin and low from fairway bunkers.	3a. Check your setup. The ball may be too far forward.
	3b. Hold your finish. There is a tendency to "help" the ball out of the trap, causing the hands to be too active and the arms to bend through impact.
4. Shots are hit "fat" in the fairway bunker.	4a. Check your setup. Ball position may be too far back.
	4b. If ball position is fine, you may be decelerating through impact.

Sand Shot Drills

1. Board Drill for the Explosion Shot

Learning to feel and use the "bounce" of your sand wedge is important in producing a high, soft explosion shot.

Bury board, 3 feet by 2 inches by 4 inches, so that it is level with the surface of the sand. Place a few balls at the end of the board for safety. On the middle-front portion of the board, make a pile of sand, and make swings hitting the sand off the board. With the clubface slightly open, you will hear and feel the club bounce off the board. Then place a ball on the pile of sand on the board and feel the club bounce off the board. The ball flies out with the sand. Finally, place a ball in a good lie in the trap and take swings from there. The focus of this drill is feeling the bounce, not controlling distance. Maintain your normal swing pace with a 4 swing length.

Success Goal = 15 total swings, feeling and hearing the club bounce off the board

    5 swings hitting sand off the board

    5 swings hitting the ball off sand on the board

    5 swings hitting the ball off the sand (good lie)

Your Score =

    (#) _____ swings hitting the sand off the board

    (#) _____ swings hitting the ball off sand on the board

    (#) _____ swings hitting the ball off the sand (good lie)

2. Low-Trajectory Shot Using a Sand Wedge

The low-trajectory shot can be hit from a good or a poor lie. Technique is the same as for the pitch and run shot, with the feet dug into the sand as in the explosion shot. Practice this shot using your normal swing pace and a 3 swing length. Alter the lie of the ball between good and poor. Note the trajectory and roll of the ball. Forwardswing length is restricted due to the impact with the sand.

Success Goal = 16 total swings, altering the lie of the ball between a good and a poor lie and noting the trajectory and roll of the ball

    5 swings from a poor lie   2 swings from a good lie

    5 swings from a good lie   1 swing from a poor lie

    2 swings from a poor lie   1 swing from a good lie

Your Score =

    (#) _____ swings from a poor lie (5)   (#) _____ swings from a good lie (2)

    (#) _____ swings from a good lie (5)   (#) _____ swing from a poor lie (1)

    (#) _____ swings from a poor lie (2)   (#) _____ swing from a good lie (1)

3. High-Trajectory Distance Control Drill

Distance control in the sand can be practiced in the same way as for the other shots. Place targets at 6, 12, 18, and 24 yards. Distance control from the sand requires practice in adjusting your swing length, your swing pace, and the amount of sand your club contacts. Be sure the ball is sitting on top of the sand (a good lie). Repeat until you can begin to match your swing length and pace for different distances.

Success Goal = 12 total shots to various distance targets

3 shots to 6-yard target

3 shots to 12-yard target

3 shots to 18-yard target

3 shots to 24-yard target

Your Score =

(#) _____ shots to 6-yard target (3)

(#) _____ shots to 12-yard target (3)

(#) _____ shots to 18-yard target (3)

(#) _____ shots to 24-yard target (3)

4. High-Trajectory Accuracy Control Drill

Once you begin to get a feel for the distance for the high-trajectory shot, relating your swing length and swing pace for a given distance, then focus also on accuracy. Repeat the distances in Drill 3, mixing up the order of your shots, and also record your accuracy for each shot that stops within 9 feet of the target.

Success Goal = 70 percent of your shots landing within 9 feet of your target

Your Score = Record the number of shots taken at each distance and the accuracy (within 9 feet of the target)

	# Shots taken	Within 9 feet	Beyond 9 feet
2 shots at 18 yards	_____	_____	_____
2 shots at 6 yards	_____	_____	_____
2 shots at 12 yards	_____	_____	_____
2 shots at 24 yards	_____	_____	_____
1 shot at 6 yards	_____	_____	_____
1 shot at 18 yards	_____	_____	_____
1 shot at 12 yards	_____	_____	_____
1 shot at 24 yards	_____	_____	_____
Total	_____	_____	_____
Percentage	_____	_____	_____

5. Low-Trajectory Distance Control Drill

Low-trajectory shots are more difficult to control from a poor lie than from a good lie, because of the unpredictability of the depth of sand with each lie. However, with practice you begin to more accurately predict the amount of swing length and pace you need to gain distance control.

Using the same distance markers as in Drills 3 and 4 (6, 12, 18, and 24 yards), practice the low-trajectory shot from good and poor lies using a sand wedge (SW).

Success Goal = 24 total balls hit to various distance targets from good and poor lies; hit 3 shots from the good lie, followed by 3 shots from the poor lie for each distance (6, 12, 18, and 24 yards)

Your Score = Number of shots hit from both good and poor lies

	From good lie	From poor lie
3 shots at 6 yards	_____	_____
3 shots at 12 yards	_____	_____
3 shots at 18 yards	_____	_____
3 shots at 24 yards	_____	_____

6. Low-Trajectory Accuracy Control Drill

You will often have buried lies for which you will simply hope to get out of the trap and somewhere onto the green. But try for accuracy for most of your buried lies.

Accuracy on low-trajectory shots from good lies is more predictable. Note the difference in the accuracy goal for the good lie (70 percent) versus the poor lie (in which you may be content with 50 percent accuracy). As you practice and become more comfortable with the shots, increase your accuracy goals.

Success Goal = Hit shots from good and poor lies to observe the differences in accuracy and distance control; alternate good and poor lies for each of the following distances, and record your ability to land within 12 feet of your target

a. 70 percent of your shots from a good lie, stopping within 12 feet of your target

b. 50 percent of your shots from a poor lie, stopping within 12 feet of your target

Your Score = Number of shots hit toward targets at each of the following distances, alternating from good and poor lies; specify if the shot landed inside or outside of the 12-foot-wide target area

	From good lie		From poor lie	
	Outside	Inside	Outside	Inside
2 shots at 18 yards	_____	_____	_____	_____
2 shots at 6 yards	_____	_____	_____	_____
2 shots at 12 yards	_____	_____	_____	_____
2 shots at 24 yards	_____	_____	_____	_____
1 shot at 6 yards	_____	_____	_____	_____
1 shot at 18 yards	_____	_____	_____	_____
1 shot at 24 yards	_____	_____	_____	_____
1 shot at 12 yards	_____	_____	_____	_____
Total	_____	_____	_____	_____
Percentage	_____	_____	_____	_____

7. Fairway Bunker Drill

The lie of the ball determines your options. If the ball is buried, play for a safe shot. If the ball has a good lie, consider the amount of lip and the ball's distance from it. Practice hitting shots with both irons and woods from a good lie.

Success Goal = 16 total shots hit with a 6-iron and fairway wood from a good lie, with 75 percent of the shots hit successfully from the trap

5 shots with a 6-iron   2 shots with a fairway wood

5 shots with a fairway wood   1 shot with a 6-iron

2 shots with a 6-iron   1 shot with a fairway wood

Your Score =

a. (#) _____ successful shots with a 6-iron

(%) _____ successful shots with a 6-iron

b. (#) _____ successful shots with a fairway wood

(%) _____ successful shots with a fairway wood

8. On-Course Sand Drills

You will often face the following situations on the course. Try to visualize each situation and respond to the questions.

Situation A:

On a par 3, 150-yard hole, you have hit your tee shot into a greenside bunker. The pin is 10 yards from the near edge of the trap. The ball is buried under the lip of the trap.

a

Success Goal = Respond to the following questions for Situation A

1. What are your options for the next shot?
2. Indicate your shot choice and the club you would use.

Your Score = Answers to the questions

1. Next shot options:

a. _____

b. _____

2. Your shot choice (a) and club selection (b):

a. _____

b. _____

Situation B:

Your second shot on a par 5, 500-yard hole has landed in a fairway bunker. The lie is good, and the bunker has no high lip for you to contend with on your next shot.

Success Goal = Respond to the following questions for Situation B

1. What are your options for the next shot?
2. What club would you select for each option?

b

Your Score = Answers to the questions

1. Next shot options:

   a. _____

   b. _____

2. Club selection for each option:

   a. _____

   b. _____

Situation C:

Your third shot on a par 4, 360-yard hole has landed in a greenside bunker. The lie is good. The bunker is relatively flat with no high lip between your ball and the green. The pin is 40 feet from the near edge of the green.

c

Success Goal = Respond to the following questions for Situation C

1. What are your options for the next shot?
2. What club would you select for each option?

Your Score = Answers to the questions

1. Next shot options:

   a. _____

   b. _____

2. Club selection for each option:

   a. _____

   b. _____

Sand Shot
Keys to Success Checklists

For you to be a proficient golfer, it is critical that you master the sand shot. Hitting from bunkers can be a challenging and rewarding skill to perfect. The lie of the ball in the sand and the height of the bunker between the ball and the target determine the potential control for trajectory and distance of your sand shot. Once you have evaluated these factors, you are ready to determine your shot selection. The checklist items within Figures 6.3 and 6.5 can be used by your partner, teacher, or coach to evaluate your sand shots. The asterisks denote variations in the sand setup from the full swing setup.

Answers to Drill 8

Situation A

1. Next shot options:

   a. Play it as it lies—a very low percentage shot.
   b. Take an "unplayable lie" (Rule 28; 1 stroke penalty):

      • Drop the ball out of the trap, and go back to the spot where you last hit your shot.
      • Drop the ball in the trap, and go back on a straight line keeping the point of the buried lie between the ball and the pin.
      • Drop the ball in the trap within 2 club lengths of where it lies and no nearer to the hole.

2. Best option and club selection:

   a. The last two "unplayable lie" options are best, given the distance of your last shot. Assess the trap condition to get the best lie on your drop and a level stance when possible.
   b. A sand wedge is the best club for this distance, with either a good or a poor lie.

Situation B

1. Next shot options:
   Situation B, given a good lie and low lip, allows you to hit a wood or iron of your choice. Select the club that you have the most confidence in to get you into position for the next shot.
2. Club selection:
   Select the club, wood or iron, with which you feel most comfortable after practicing Drill 7.

Situation C

1. Next shot options:

   a. High trajectory
   b. Low trajectory

2. Club selection:

   a. Sand wedge (SW)
   b. Pitching wedge (PW)
   c. After practicing Drills 3 through 6, you should have developed a feel for distance and accuracy control for both the high- and low-trajectory shots from a good lie. Select the shot in which you have the most confidence.

Step 7 Advanced Putting

There are two components to putting—the putting stroke and the ability to read greens. For advanced golfers, the stroke itself should be reliable and smooth, so that the greater challenge is in learning to accurately "read the greens" and determine the influence of the green's contour on the roll of the putt.

WHY IS PUTTING IMPORTANT?

In an 18-hole round of golf, 50 percent of the strokes allotted toward par are for putting. In other words, if you would like to cut six strokes off your average score, three of those will probably come from improving your putting. Yet how many golfers spend half of their practice time putting?

HOW TO EXECUTE THE PUTTING STROKE AND READ GREENS

The putter differs greatly in physical structure from other clubs, having an almost vertical clubface that produces no loft. The putter is also shorter than other clubs and has a more upright shaft. Finding a putter that feels right for your posture and stance is extremely important.

The differences in the purpose of the stroke (to roll the ball) and the design of the club (shorter and more upright) forces you to modify both your grip and your setup position. This plus the need to "read the green," to calculate the direction and speed of the roll of the ball, make putting one of the most challenging skills in golf.

Reading the Green

If you travel and play golf, you will note primarily two different types of grass on greens, bent and bermuda. Bent grass is found more in cooler climates, and bermuda in warmer climates. Golf courses select the grass that works best for them in terms of maximum growth and durability.

These two most prominent grasses for greens are easily distinguished by appearance and texture. Bent grass is a flat, thin-bladed leaf grass that has a smooth appearance and texture when

you stroke it. Bermuda is found in hotter, more humid climates and has a more bristly, rough texture. Because of this texture and the fact that it is thick-bladed, bermuda grass has a more profound effect on the ball—the ball nestles in the blades. Bermuda also goes dormant, turning brown in the winter, causing many golf courses to overseed with rye grass to keep the greens looking green. Dormant bermuda grass may not appear as attractive as during its growing season, but it is still a playable surface.

The two grasses respond differently when you putt on them. If you applied the same stroke relative to pace and length on both greens, the ball will roll farther on the bent green than on the bermuda green. Bent grass offers less resistance to the roll of the ball because of the texture of the grass. This applies also to the amount of "break" when reading the slope of the green. The ball will break, or turn more, on bent than on bermuda, for the same amount of slope. If you are used to a particular type of grass, have patience when playing on different grass. You will have to adjust your stroke pace, so be sure to practice putting before playing in order to get the feel of the greens.

Putt With the Grain

You may have heard the phrases *putting with the grain* and *putting against the grain*. Grain is the direction in which the grass grows. When putted with the grain, the ball tends to roll faster and break more than when putted against the grain. In the early mornings when the grass has just been cut, it is difficult to determine what direction the grass grows in, and the effects of grain are minimal. In the early afternoons, as the grass grows, the grain is easier to see and feel and will have a greater effect on the roll of the ball. Figure 7.1 illustrates the effects of grain on putts relative to the direction of the putt and the direction of the grain.

There are several other cues you can use to tell the grain of the grass. You can tell by feeling the grass, but during regulation play it is illegal to run your hand across the grass to determine the grain. Most golfers use other

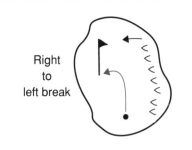

Right
to
left break

a Grain growing with the direction of the putt enhances break

b Grain growing against the direction of the putt lessens break

(< = direction of the grain in the green)

Figure 7.1 Grain growing with the direction of the putt enhances break (a); grain growing against the direction of the putt lessens break (b).

visual techniques to help them determine the direction of the grain: the color of the grass, the growth pattern around the hole or cup, the presence of water, and the direction of the prevailing wind.

When you look at the grass from one side of the cup, it will appear dark, and from the opposite side, light and shiny. When the grass you are putting into appears dark to you, you are putting into, or against, the grain. The putt will be slower and will have less than normal distance. In contrast, when you putt with the grain, into grass that appears shiny to you, the putt will be faster and will go farther.

It is also possible to tell the grain or nap of the green by looking at the edge of the hole. One side of the cutout hole will normally appear clean and neat while the other side will have exposed roots and a more ragged look. If the cup hasn't been cut recently, you can actually see the growth of the grass over the edge of one side, whereas the other side will be darker and bare of blades of grass where the roots are exposed. The grain of the grass is running toward the ragged, bare side of the hole.

Grass also tends to grow toward water and in the direction of the prevailing wind. If there is a stream or water hazard nearby, the green will probably grow toward that source of water. If you have no idea of the grain of the green, either play it "true," as if there were no grain, or use the farmer's standby that the grass grows toward the setting sun (west).

Fast or Slow Greens

Other conditions also affect putting besides the type of grass. As you walk on a green, you can get a feel for the surface. Greens that feel firm tend to be faster than ones that feel soft. Wind tends to dry out the greens, making them faster. Wet conditions from rain or watering systems tend to make the greens slower. Greens that have been cut in the morning are faster than in the afternoon, when the grass has had an opportunity to grow. Alertness to these conditions can help you make minor adjustments in your stroke pace or length as needed. See Table 7.1 for a summary of influences that affect a putt's speed.

Table 7.1 Influences on the Speed of a Putt

Factors	Fast conditions	Slow conditions
Type of grass	Bent	Bermuda
Direction of grain	With	Against
Green surface	Hard	Soft
Time of day	Morning	Afternoon
Climatic conditions	Dry or Windy	Wet

Reading the Slope of the Green

When you "read" a green, you are getting a picture of any undulations, the grain of the grass, and the speed of the surface. You should begin to read the green as you walk up to it. Observe the high and low sides, and note whether there are any ridges or mounds, slants or low spots, in the green's surface.

Every green is designed to drain off water. So in most cases the water will run toward some drain, stream, or lake, and you can assume that the green will be slightly sloped in that direction. Similarly, if you play in an area where there are mountains on one side of the course, be aware that the greens generally will slope away from the mountains.

It is also a good idea to stand on the downhill side of the slope and look at the line of travel for your putt. This angle of view will give you a good idea of how much your putt will break.

Plumb-Bobbing Technique

Some golfers also use a technique referred to as plumb bobbing. In this technique, the putter is held an arm's length away from the body (see Figure 7.2), feet are about shoulder-width apart, and weight is evenly distributed on both feet. Individuals who are right-eye dominant close the left eye and hold up the putter between the thumb and forefinger of the left hand. The arm is kept extended in front, and the putter is allowed to hang so it can swing freely. With the right eye, the shaft of the putter is aligned with the ball; then one looks up the shaft toward the hole. If the shaft appears to be directly on the hole, the putt is straight. If the shaft appears to be left of the hole, the ball will break right. Similarly, if the shaft is on the right of the hole, the putt will break to the left.

Although many golfers use this plumb-bobbing technique, it tends *not to be accurate*. So trust your eyes and read the greens as previously described.

Figure 7.2 Plumb bobbing technique.

PUTTING STRATEGY

Par for each hole is based on the assumption that most golfers will use two putts on each hole. With this in mind, it is important to determine how you want to use your putts. Just as good billiard players determine not only where they want to hit the ball but also where the ball will end up, so too must the golfer.

If you find yourself putting downhill from above the hole, you should consider where you want your ball to go if you happen to miss the putt. A downhill putt will often result in a long roll past the hole if you hit the putt too firmly. That is why most golfers consider a downhill putt much more difficult than an uphill putt.

If you have an extreme downhill putt, you must putt with less pace, because it will give way to the ball and soften the putter's impact on the ball. We suggest that you always play the ball in the sweet spot of the putter and use less pace (less backswing distance and/or slower motion).

The time to think about your putting strategy is really before you hit your approach shot. In general, most golfers prefer to putt from below the hole, so they aim to leave their approach shots on the low side of the green.

Knowing when to "lag" a putt and when to go for ("charge") the hole is also important. If you have a birdie-range putt but it is downhill on a fast green, it may be wiser to lag (be cautious and get the ball close to the hole) rather than take the chance of rolling 8 or 10 feet past the hole.

THE PUTTING STROKE

The grip for the putt places the club more in the palms of the hands, rather than in the fingers as in the full swing grip. Place the putter face behind the ball square to the desired target, with the bottom of the club flat on the ground. The shape of the bottom of the club, and its relationship to the angle of the shaft, should be compatible with your posture. The correct posture should allow your eyes to be directly over or slightly behind the ball but on the target line. Arms hang from the shoulders, and your weight should be evenly distributed across a square alignment. The ball should be positioned slightly to the target side of center.

The putting stroke motion is pendular. The club, hands, and arms work as a unit. The upper and lower body are still, but not rigid, during the stroke. The backswing and forwardswing are equal in length. The stroke is smooth and continuous, back and then through the ball.

Advanced players use the same fundamentals as beginners for the putting stroke. However, advanced players have putting strokes that are *more repeatable and consistent* day after day, and they adapt better to a variety of green conditions. Figure 7.3, a-d, illustrates three putting stroke styles commonly seen in good players. The bent arm position (left column) allows the player to use the arms only or a combination of arms and shoulders as a unit. The more extended arm position (right column) provides for the arms and shoulders as a unit and is not effective if only the arms are used. The "crosshanded" (or, more appropriately, "target hand low") position (center column) provides for an arm and shoulder unit that additionally limits any activity in the hands. Some players tend to get very hand oriented in putting and find this style particularly beneficial.

Figure 7.3 Keys to Success:
Three Putting Positions
(*indicates variation from basic full swing motion)

**Preparation
Phase**

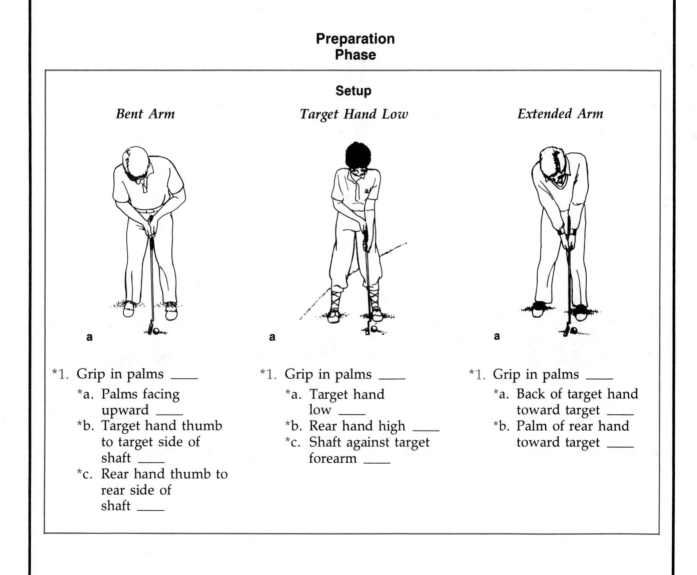

Setup

Bent Arm — *Target Hand Low* — *Extended Arm*

a — a — a

*1. Grip in palms ____
  *a. Palms facing upward ____
  *b. Target hand thumb to target side of shaft ____
  *c. Rear hand thumb to rear side of shaft ____

*1. Grip in palms ____
  *a. Target hand low ____
  *b. Rear hand high ____
  *c. Shaft against target forearm ____

*1. Grip in palms ____
  *a. Back of target hand toward target ____
  *b. Palm of rear hand toward target ____

Bent Arm

2. Feet shoulder-width apart ____
3. Weight even ____
4. Posture flat back ____
*5. Eyes over target line ____
6. Ball forward of center ____
7. Square alignment
   a. Shoulders ____
   b. Hips ____
   c. Feet ____
8. Square blade ____

Target Hand Low

2. Feet shoulder-width apart ____
3. Weight even ____
4. Posture flat back ____
*5. Eyes over target line ____
*6. Ball off target heel ____
7. Square alignment ____
   a. Shoulders ____
   b. Hips ____
   c. Feet ____
8. Square blade ____

Extended Arm

2. Feet shoulder-width apart ____
3. Weight even ____
4. Posture flat back ____
*5. Eyes over target line ____
*6. Ball off target heel ____
7. Square alignment ____
   a. Shoulders ____
   b. Hips ____
   c. Feet ____
8. Square blade ____

Execution Phase

Backswing

Bent Arm

Target Hand Low

Extended Arm

b

b

b

*1. Arms, hands, shoulders, and putter swing as unit ____
*2. Hips still ____
*3. Backswing length 1, 2, or 3 ____

*1. Arms, hands, shoulders, and putter swing as unit ____
*2. Hips still ____
*3. Backswing length 1, 2, or 3 ____

*1. Arms, hands, shoulders, and putter swing as unit ____
*2. Hips still ____
*3. Backswing length 1, 2, or 3 ____

Forwardswing

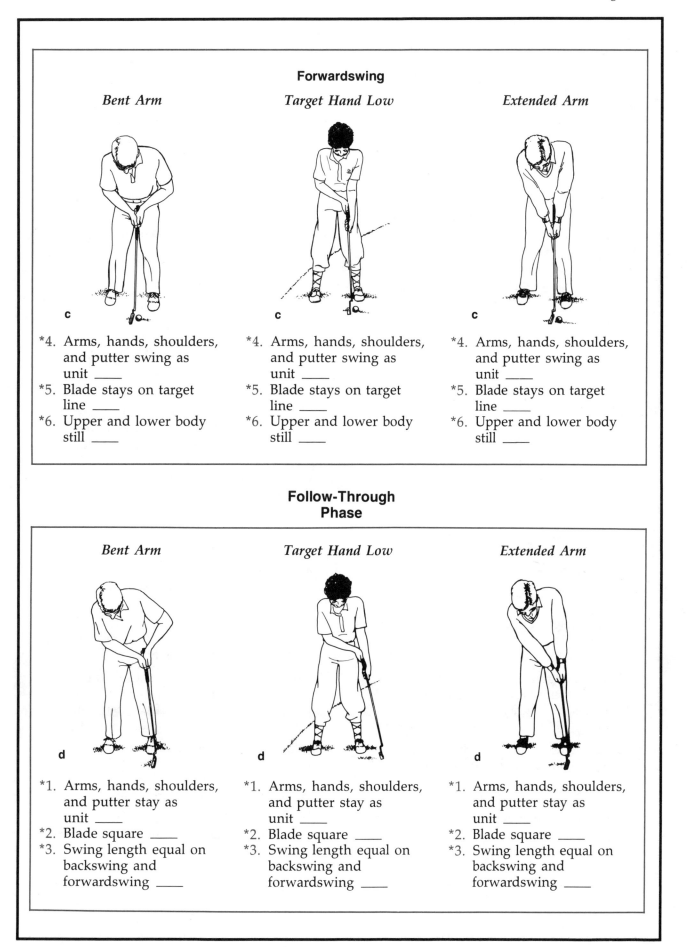

Bent Arm	Target Hand Low	Extended Arm

c

*4. Arms, hands, shoulders, and putter swing as unit ____
*5. Blade stays on target line ____
*6. Upper and lower body still ____

c

*4. Arms, hands, shoulders, and putter swing as unit ____
*5. Blade stays on target line ____
*6. Upper and lower body still ____

c

*4. Arms, hands, shoulders, and putter swing as unit ____
*5. Blade stays on target line ____
*6. Upper and lower body still ____

Follow-Through Phase

Bent Arm	Target Hand Low	Extended Arm

d

*1. Arms, hands, shoulders, and putter stay as unit ____
*2. Blade square ____
*3. Swing length equal on backswing and forwardswing ____

d

*1. Arms, hands, shoulders, and putter stay as unit ____
*2. Blade square ____
*3. Swing length equal on backswing and forwardswing ____

d

*1. Arms, hands, shoulders, and putter stay as unit ____
*2. Blade square ____
*3. Swing length equal on backswing and forwardswing ____

ALIGNMENT TIPS

As in your other strokes, be sure to align your putts—all putts. There is one advantage in putting rules that is helpful in lining up your putts —you are allowed to mark and clean your ball. When replacing the ball on the putting surface, many players align the label of the ball in the direction they want the ball to roll. For example, if you are using a Titleist golf ball, align the word *Titleist* so that the lettering goes down the desired line of roll (see Figure 7.4). Remember, you can touch the ball only if you have marked it first!

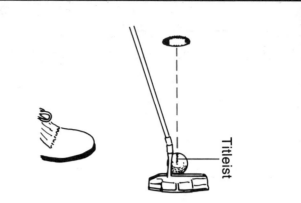

Figure 7.4   Aligning the club with the brand name label of the ball.

Detecting Putting Errors

Errors in putting fall into four categories: technique, distance, direction, and green reading. Both advanced and beginning players can have errors in all four. Work on your technique, because errors in the other three can often be traced to technique.

ERROR 🚫

CORRECTION

ERROR	CORRECTION
1. On straight putts, ball consistently falls to the right as the ball slows down.	1. Check alignment, then club path. Club may be swinging across the line, adding sidespin rather than overspin.
2. On bent greens, the ball always rolls far past the hole, but distance is good on bermuda greens.	2. Bent greens are faster, and an adjustment in your swing pace or swing length (or both) is needed when you go from bent to bermuda and vice versa.
3. On right-to-left putts, the ball does not begin to curve until past the hole.	3. Check your swing pace and swing length for the distance. The ball does not curve until it slows down, so you may be putting the ball too fast.
4. On bermuda greens, the ball does not break as much as predicted.	4. Check the direction of the grain; it may either exaggerate or diminish the normal break (review Figure 7.1).

ERROR	CORRECTION
5. On downhill putts, the ball consistently misses to the left of the hole (for right-handed putter).	5. You are probably not setting up properly, resulting in putts that are not aimed correctly. Be sure that your eyes are directly over the target line during the setup. Also check to be sure you are not pulling the putt.

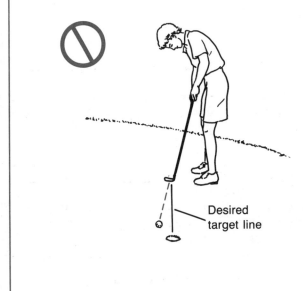

Desired
target line

Putting Drills

1. Putting Line Drill With Eyes Closed

The line drill is used to practice putting short putts and controlling the length of your backswing. It is also good for learning to "trust" your stroke by practicing with your eyes closed.

Place six balls at 6-inch intervals on a target line to the hole. The first ball from the hole is about 1 foot away from the hole. Starting with the ball closest to the hole, putt the balls into the hole with your eyes closed. When a putt is missed, start again with all six balls.

Success Goal = 5 repetitions of making 6 consecutive putts with your eyes closed

Your Score =

    a. (#) _____ putts made out of 6

    b. (#) _____ putts made out of 6

    c. (#) _____ putts made out of 6

    d. (#) _____ putts made out of 6

    e. (#) _____ putts made out of 6

2. *Apron Putting Drill*

The apron or ''fringe''—the slightly longer cut grass surrounding the green—can provide an excellent distance target for putting. This drill will help you learn to control the distance on your putts and to identify your natural tendency in distance control. It is a good warm-up before playing and allows you to get the feel of the greens. You won't be putting to a hole, because your focus should be on distance control, not on ''making the putt.''

Using four balls, place each ball on the green so that it must be stroked a different distance to the apron of the green. Each stroke is independent of the other. For example, if you putt the first ball and it comes up short, you don't necessarily want to hit the next ball harder. Many professional golfers talk about hitting the first putt on each green for distance and the second putt for ''money.'' Treat each of these balls as if it were your first putt on a green.

Success Goal = 12 total putts: 3 repetitions using 4 balls each time, recording how many are short of the fringe, on the fringe, or beyond where the fringe starts (consider long or short by 6 or more inches)

Your Score = Record the putt distances

Putt Number	Long	Fringe	Short
1	_____	_____	_____
2	_____	_____	_____
3	_____	_____	_____
4	_____	_____	_____
5	_____	_____	_____
6	_____	_____	_____
7	_____	_____	_____
8	_____	_____	_____
9	_____	_____	_____
10	_____	_____	_____
11	_____	_____	_____
12	_____	_____	_____
Total	_____	_____	_____
Percentage	_____	_____	_____

3. *Putting Bias Correction Drill*

If you found, in doing Drill 2, that you have a decided bias toward long or short putts, repeat Drill 2 with the following focus. If your bias is toward leaving your putts short, select a spot 6 or 7 inches beyond the fringe and putt to that spot. If you tend to normally go past the fringe, select a spot short of the fringe. In time you will begin to improve your distance control. If you have no bias, move to Drill 4 or repeat Drill 2.

Success Goal = 12 total putts: 3 repetitions using 4 balls each time, determining percentage of putts short of the fringe, on the fringe, or beyond the fringe (long) (compare to Drill 2)

Your Score = Record the putt distances

Putt Number	Long	Fringe	Short
1	_____	_____	_____
2	_____	_____	_____
3	_____	_____	_____
4	_____	_____	_____
5	_____	_____	_____
6	_____	_____	_____
7	_____	_____	_____
8	_____	_____	_____
9	_____	_____	_____
10	_____	_____	_____
11	_____	_____	_____
12	_____	_____	_____
Total	_____	_____	_____
Percentage	_____	_____	_____

Comparison to Drill 2

	Long	Fringe	Short
Drill 2 (percentage)	_____	_____	_____
Drill 3 (percentage)	_____	_____	_____

4. *On-Course Distance Putting*

Keep track of your putts for two rounds, noting the number of putts that are long, on target, and short. Then use this information to continue working on your distance control.

Success Goal = Keep track of your putts for 2 rounds, recording how many are long, on target, or short

Your Score = Record the putting distances and calculate distance biases

	Long	On target	Short
Round 1	_____	_____	_____
Round 2	_____	_____	_____
Total	_____	_____	_____
Percentage	_____	_____	_____

5. On-Course Situations Drill

Consider the following on-course situations and respond to the questions.

Situation A:

Your tee time was 7:00 a.m., and you are on the 5th hole. You are 20 feet from the pin, on a bermuda green. The grain is growing toward the ball from the hole. What are your thoughts in preparing for this putt?

Success Goal = Write out your thoughts on preparing for the putt (consider the time, grass type, grain, etc.)

Your Score = Write out your thoughts

_____

_____

_____

Situation B:

You have a right-to-left-breaking putt on bent grass. The grain is growing from right to left. There was a rain shower 15 minutes earlier. What are your thoughts in preparing to stroke this putt?

Success Goal = Write out your thoughts on preparing for this putt

Your Score = Write out your thoughts

_____

_____

_____

Situation C:

You are putting on a two-level green that is relatively flat on the first level. Your ball rests on the lower level, and you must putt about 20 feet up onto the higher level. What effect will the second level have on the speed and direction of your putt? What would happen if you were putting from the upper level to the lower level?

Success Goal = Write out your answers to the questions

Your Score = Your answers to the questions

_____

_____

_____

Advanced Putting
Keys to Success Checklist

Putting is one of the most challenging aspects of golf. All great golfers practice their putting extensively and often kid about changing putters and styles. However, all great golfers decide on one technique and stick with it until such time as they consciously decide to learn (and practice) a new style. You should never change in the middle of a round or tournament.

The checklist in Figure 7.3 can be used by you or your golf professional or a trained observer to evaluate your progress. Be sure to always check your alignment and posture for good putting technique.

Answers to Drill 5

Situation A

1. Consider external elements

   a. Type of grass: Bermuda grass will be slower than bent grass.
   b. Time and degree of wetness: 7 a.m. may be wet; grass could have just been cut.
   c. Grain of grass: If putt is against the grain, must hit it firmer.
   d. Firmness of green: Unknown, but may be soft.

2. Consider your biases.
3. Decide _where_ you would like to be if you miss the putt. (Be careful that you perceive this as good planning and not a self-doubt.)

Situation B

1. Consider external elements

   a. Type of grass: Bent grass is usually faster.
   b. Grain of grass: Right to left—so putt will naturally break that direction.
   c. Degree of slope: Breaks right to left (will combine with grain direction to be even greater right-to-left break).
   d. Rain: Will make the ball go slower (lessens the impact of the grain).

2. Consider your biases.
3. Decide where you want to leave the putt.

Situation C

1. Consider external elements

   a. If putting _up_ to the second level, must use more force.
   b. If putt is perpendicular to break in level, it will not affect direction.
   c. If putt up at an angle across level, the ball will break toward the lower side.
   d. If putt from upper to lower level, putt will be faster.

2. Consider your biases.
3. Decide where you want to leave the putt.

Step 8   Challenge Shots

During a round of golf, not all shots land in the fairway or on the green. Perhaps you have already experienced a shot or two from under the bushes or next to a tree. In these situations, you can take an unplayable lie and get relief, counting a one-stroke penalty, or you can go for it!

The shots you will learn in this step are called challenge shots. Hopefully you won't have to call on them too often, but they are nice to know just in case.

WHY ARE CHALLENGE SHOTS IMPORTANT?

Every golfer from time to time finds a ball under a tree or bush, or nestled next to a tree trunk, and even in an unplayable lie in bushes. Up till now you've probably taken a one-stroke penalty because it seemed frivolous to try to hit it from an obstructed location. Not any more. These shots are fun! Any time you can advance the ball toward the target *and* back into play, give it a try. You have shortened the distance for your next shot and saved a stroke on an unplayable lie, which may or may not provide you with a good position for the next shot.

How to Execute Challenge Shots

In this section you will learn five shots. The shots do not have particular names, but are described in terms of the situation or execution. With practice you can become fairly proficient at executing them and have some fun. These shots are fun to practice and most rewarding when used successfully on the course. And true to their label, they are a challenge!

Knees Shot

The knees shot is used when hitting from under trees. This type of situation is illustrated in the left column of Figure 8.1. In executing this shot, use your regular setup position, but on your knees. The ball position is toward the center. With practice you can establish the ideal ball position for your swing. Your swing motion is more like a baseball swing. You will feel like you are swinging *around* your body. A wood is best to use in this shot because the desired ball trajectory is low, and the angle of approach is shallow.

Modified Knees Shot

A modification of the knees shot is illustrated in the center column of Figure 8.1. This shot is a better choice if the tree limbs are higher. Lower your body by widening your stance and flexing your knees (as your stance widens, your knees turn in for support). This position lets you get closer to the ground and under the limbs, yet create a steeper angle of approach than in the knees shot. An iron or a wood may be used— select the club that allows you to hit safely from under the tree.

Tree Shot

Believe it or not, the shot illustrated in the right column of Figure 8.1 has occurred frequently during play. The ball lodges precariously on a limb. Note the similarity between this shot and the knees shot. You're standing rather than on your knees, but the swing motion is the same as the knee shot—around your body like a baseball swing. You can use either an iron or wood. Care must be taken not to move the limb in addressing the ball. If you cause the ball to dislodge before you swing, there is a one-stroke penalty, and the ball is replayed (Rule 18.2).

Figure 8.1 Keys to Success:
Knees and Tree Shots

(*indicates variation from the normal swing)

**Preparation
Phase**

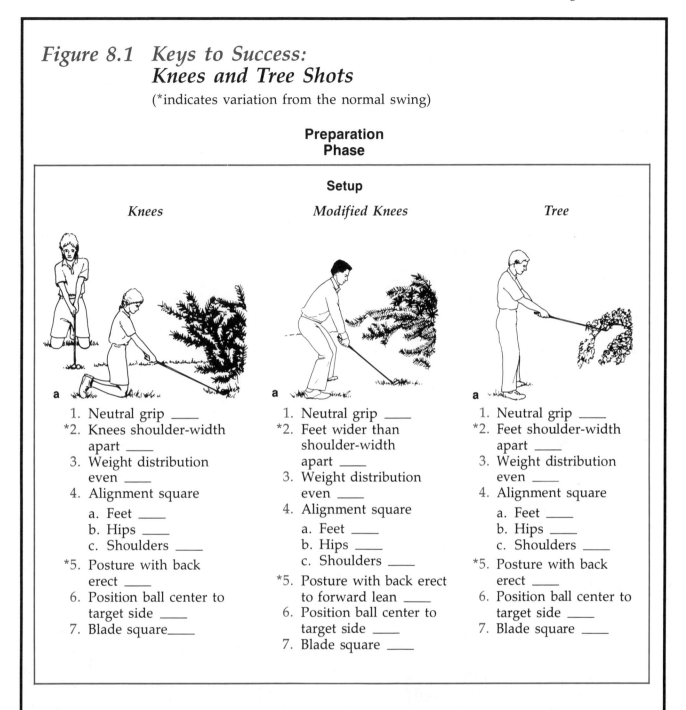

Setup

Knees   *Modified Knees*   *Tree*

Knees
1. Neutral grip ____
*2. Knees shoulder-width apart ____
3. Weight distribution even ____
4. Alignment square
  a. Feet ____
  b. Hips ____
  c. Shoulders ____
*5. Posture with back erect ____
6. Position ball center to target side ____
7. Blade square____

Modified Knees
1. Neutral grip ____
*2. Feet wider than shoulder-width apart ____
3. Weight distribution even ____
4. Alignment square
  a. Feet ____
  b. Hips ____
  c. Shoulders ____
*5. Posture with back erect to forward lean ____
6. Position ball center to target side ____
7. Blade square ____

Tree
1. Neutral grip ____
*2. Feet shoulder-width apart ____
3. Weight distribution even ____
4. Alignment square
  a. Feet ____
  b. Hips ____
  c. Shoulders ____
*5. Posture with back erect ____
6. Position ball center to target side ____
7. Blade square ____

Execution
Phase

Backswing

Knees   *Modified Knees*   *Tree*

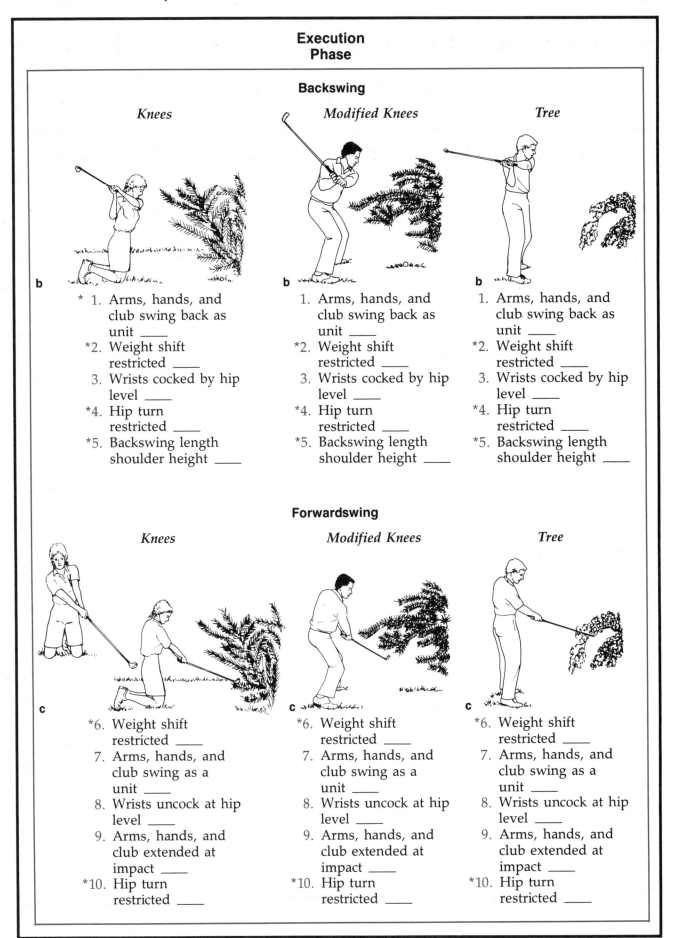

b

* 1. Arms, hands, and club swing back as unit ____
*2. Weight shift restricted ____
 3. Wrists cocked by hip level ____
*4. Hip turn restricted ____
*5. Backswing length shoulder height ____

b

 1. Arms, hands, and club swing back as unit ____
*2. Weight shift restricted ____
 3. Wrists cocked by hip level ____
*4. Hip turn restricted ____
*5. Backswing length shoulder height ____

b

 1. Arms, hands, and club swing back as unit ____
*2. Weight shift restricted ____
 3. Wrists cocked by hip level ____
*4. Hip turn restricted ____
*5. Backswing length shoulder height ____

Forwardswing

Knees   *Modified Knees*   *Tree*

c

*6. Weight shift restricted ____
 7. Arms, hands, and club swing as a unit ____
 8. Wrists uncock at hip level ____
 9. Arms, hands, and club extended at impact ____
*10. Hip turn restricted ____

c

*6. Weight shift restricted ____
 7. Arms, hands, and club swing as a unit ____
 8. Wrists uncock at hip level ____
 9. Arms, hands, and club extended at impact ____
*10. Hip turn restricted ____

c

*6. Weight shift restricted ____
 7. Arms, hands, and club swing as a unit ____
 8. Wrists uncock at hip level ____
 9. Arms, hands, and club extended at impact ____
*10. Hip turn restricted ____

Follow-Through Phase

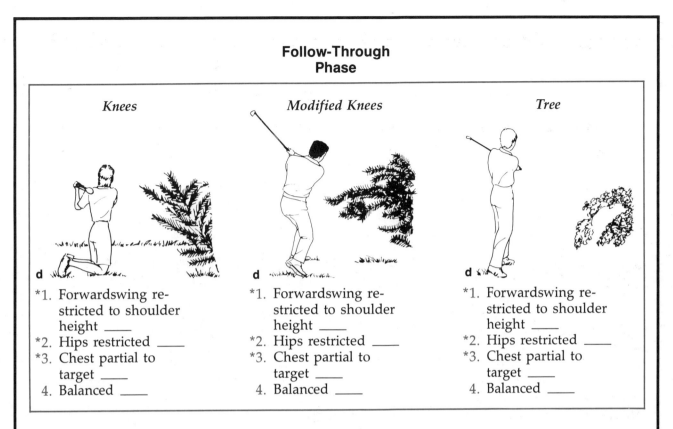

| *Knees* | *Modified Knees* | *Tree* |

*1. Forwardswing restricted to shoulder height ____
*2. Hips restricted ____
*3. Chest partial to target ____
4. Balanced ____

*1. Forwardswing restricted to shoulder height ____
*2. Hips restricted ____
*3. Chest partial to target ____
4. Balanced ____

*1. Forwardswing restricted to shoulder height ____
*2. Hips restricted ____
*3. Chest partial to target ____
4. Balanced ____

Backward Shot

This shot is useful when the ball comes to rest near a tree or obstruction and a regular swing is not possible. The situation illustrated in Figure 8.2 is common. You can get a backswing, but the ball is too close to the tree to get set up.

Figure 8.2 Backward shot situation.

To execute this shot, you set up with your back to the target. The ball is positioned from the ankle forward toward your toes and 2 or 3 inches outside the foot. Your ideal position can be obtained through practice swings, noting where the club clips the grass. The clubface is aligned toward the target, and the club is gripped with the palm of the rear hand facing the target. The swing motion uses *no wrists*. The club is an extension of the arm. A sequence of the swing motion for the backward shot is illustrated in Figure 8.3, a-d.

Note in Figure 8.3c that the *body bends* on the forwardswing. This is important, to reduce any stress on the shoulder joint. Go through the motion several times at a slow speed to get the desired synchronization of the movement. You can achieve surprising distance and control with this shot.

Figure 8.3 Keys to Success:
   Backward Shot

**Preparation
Phase**

Setup

1. Back to target ____
2. Grip with palm of rear hand facing target ____
3. Blade square (toe pointing toward rear ankle) ____
4. Club and rear arm in a straight line ____
5. Feet shoulder-width apart ____
6. Weight distribution even ____
7. Ball position from the ankle forward to the toes ____
8. Slight bend at the thighs ____

**Execution
Phase**

Backswing

1. Club and rear arm swing back (up) as unit ____
2. No wrist motion ____
3. Swing length:

   a. Parallel to ground ____
   b. Perpendicular to ground ____

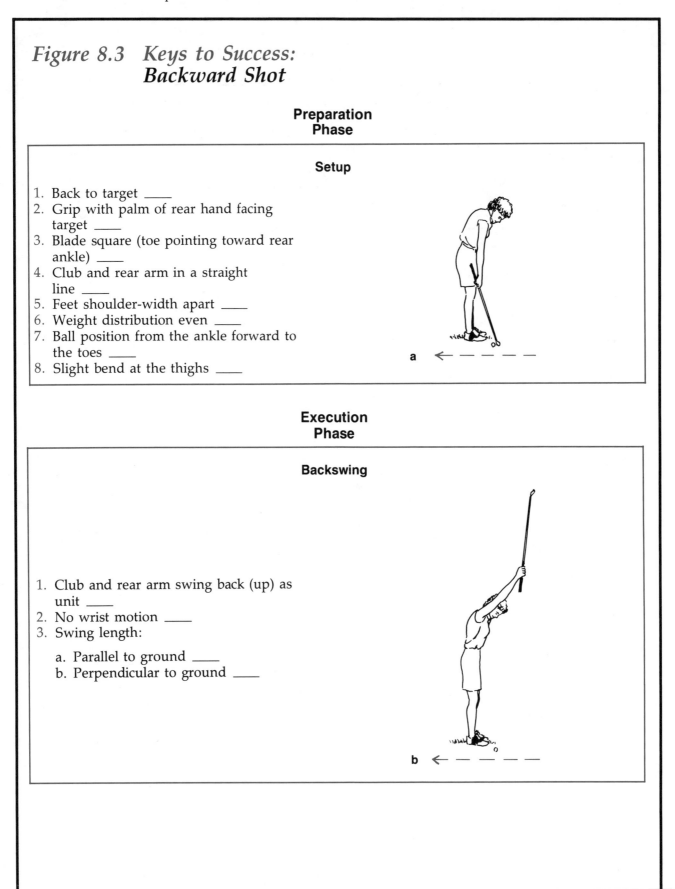

Forwardswing

1. Club and rear arm swing as unit ____
2. No wrist movement ____
3. Body bends forward just prior to ball contact ____

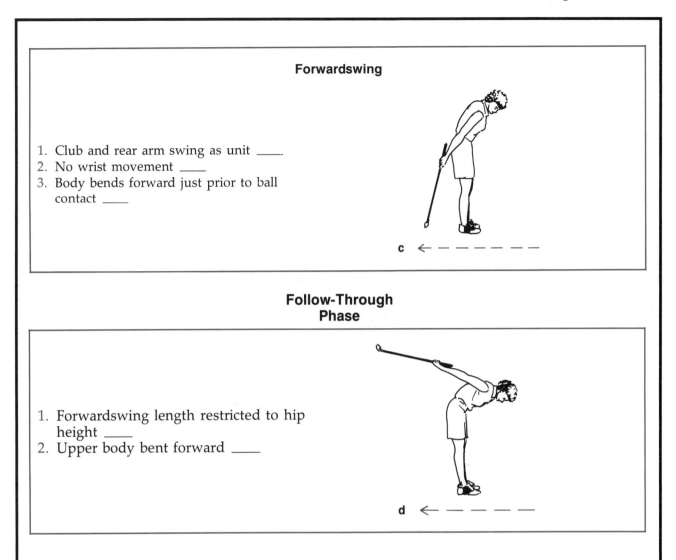

c ← — — — — —

Follow-Through Phase

1. Forwardswing length restricted to hip height ____
2. Upper body bent forward ____

d ← — — — —

Modified Backward Shot

Another technique is to use the backside of the club and swing in reverse. It's not as difficult

Figure 8.4 Modified backward shot.

as it might seem—your mind and body adapt very well with a bit of practice. Be sure to reverse your grip, with the rear hand below the target hand (see Figure 8.4).

This modified backward shot can be used for short distances, when you are trying to get the ball back into play. Often only a chip shot is needed. The shot is most effective close to the green when the ball is next to a tree and a conventional shot is impossible.

Use the same technique as your normal shots, just in reverse. Experiment with different clubs to find one you are most comfortable with (a putter design with a straight shaft as illustrated in the appendix Figure A.3a is very effective). Avoid using the shot without practice.

Detecting Challenge Shot Errors

The challenge shots presented here are not difficult. Errors on the course are usually a result of excitement. Everyone wants to see if the shots have worked before they've been fully executed. Be sure to practice them enough to develop your confidence before using them in competition.

ERROR    **CORRECTION**

ERROR	CORRECTION
1. You hit consistently behind the ball in practicing the knee shot.	1. Practice Drill 1. There is a tendency to drop the rear shoulder on the forward swing causing the mis-hit.
2. On the course the knee shot is topped.	2. Practice Drill 1. The upper body may be moving laterally on the forwardswing rather than turning.
3. The backward shot is hit fat.	3. This can have three causes. The wrist may be active, the ball position may be too far toward the heel, or the arm swing and body motion may be out of sync. Practice Drill 5 to systematically determine the cause.
4. The ball is ''whiffed'' during practice of the backward shot.	4. The tendency in hitting the backward shot is to get too wristy. Practice Drill 5 to feel the arm motion and body swing.
5. The ball is ''whiffed'' during practice of the tree shot.	5. The rear shoulder is also a cause in mis-hits in the tree shot. Practice Drill 4 to feel the level swing motion.

Challenge Shot Drills

When practicing these drills, try to visualize situations in which they would be used. Between each drill, hit five balls with your normal swing.

1. Knees Shot Drill

Practice this shot initially with the ball on a tee. Use a fairway wood. Make three practice swings between each ball to feel the motion. Note the ball flight and distance the ball travels. Have a friend hold a club to represent a tree or branch as illustrated.

Success Goal = 15 total shots, with 3 practice swings in between, using a fairway wood

5 balls teed

5 balls on the ground

2 balls teed

3 balls on the ground

Your Score =

(#) ____ balls hit teed (5)

(#) ____ balls hit on the ground (5)

(#) ____ balls hit teed (2)

(#) ____ balls hit on the ground (3)

2. Knees Shot Drill for Accuracy

Repeat Drill 1, focusing on accuracy. Select a target between 50 and 75 yards away. Adjust the target yardages to meet your distances. Hit all the balls from the ground. Remember to work on your alignment when going for a specific target or place a club on the ground for an alignment aid.

Success Goal = 15 total shots, hitting 75 percent within 15 yards of the target

Your Score =

a. (#) ____ ball hits

b. (#) ____ balls hit within 15 yards of target

c. (%) ____ accuracy (b ÷ a)

3. Modified Knees Shot

Use a driver and select a target between 50 and 75 yards away. Focus on accuracy. Adjust your target lengths as you gain greater control. Repeat using other clubs.

Success Goal = 15 total shots, hitting 75 percent within 15 yards of the target; calculate your accuracy percentage

Your Score =

a. (#) _____ balls hit

b. (#) _____ balls hit within 15 yards of target

c. (%) _____ accuracy (b÷a)

4. Tree Shot Drill

This shot requires a horizontal swing motion similar to the swing for the knees shot. It is a rare shot, but it can happen. So, familiarize yourself with the swing motion by imagining that your ball landed on the limbs of a bush. Practice making swings with your 7-iron, then with a fairway wood, through the imagined ball's location. This is like tee-ball, a preliminary game to baseball.

Success Goal = 20 total practice swings

10 swings with a 7-iron

10 swings with a fairway wood

Your Score =

a. (#) _____ swings with a 7-iron

b. (#) _____ swings with a fairway wood

5. Backward Shot Drill

Review the setup position and swing motion before practicing. Make practice swings to determine your ball position. Be sure to allow your body to bend on the forwardswing. Select an initial target 50 to 75 yards away. Then adjust the target to your distances. Practice with a variety of irons. Begin with a 7-iron. Make slow swings until you feel the coordination of the movement.

Success Goal = 15 total shots using a 7-iron, hitting 75 percent toward the target

Your Score =

a. (#) _____ balls hit (15)

b. (#) _____ balls hit toward the target

c. (%) _____ accuracy (b÷a)

6. Modified Backward Shot Drill

The distance potential of this shot is less than for the backward shot. However, it is a good shot to know. Make practice swings until you feel comfortable with the motion. Hit balls on the tee initially. Then hit from the ground. Select a target 20 to 30 yards away, and start with an 8-iron.

Success Goal = 15 total shots using an 8-iron, hitting 50 percent toward the target

7 balls hit from a tee

8 balls hit from the ground

Your Score =

a. (#) ____ balls hit (15)

b. (#) ____ balls hit toward the target

c. (%) ____ accuracy (b ÷ a)

7. Drills for On-Course Applications of Challenge Shots

Challenge shots come up infrequently on the course. However, when the situations do arise, you can save strokes by knowing some of these alternative strategies. During your practice rounds, create opportunities to apply these shots.

Success Goal = 10 total challenge shots practiced on the course

2 knee shots

2 modified knees shots

2 tree shots

2 backward shots

2 modified backward shots

Your Score =

(#) ____ knees shots (2)

(#) ____ modified knees shots (2)

(#) ____ tree shots (2)

(#) ____ backward shots (2)

(#) ____ modified backward shots (2)

Challenge Shots
Keys to Success Checklists

Challenge shots are fun. They will be used very infrequently on the course, compared to other shots, but in situations where you are able to use them to save a shot, you will be rewarded. Remember, you need to practice them first before trying them on the course. The checklists in Figures 8.1 and 8.3 can be used by your partner, teacher, or coach to evaluate your challenge shots. The asterisks denote differences between the challenge shots and your full swing motion.

Step 9 Understanding Playing Conditions

What do you think of as "ideal" weather conditions for playing golf? You may like to play in any conditions—hot, rain, cold, even snow. Or maybe you like to play only on days with mild temperatures, low humidity, and lots of sunshine. One nice aspect of golf is that most of the time you can be selective. However, you might not be playing a lot if you wait on the "ideal" conditions, and obviously, if you are competing, you have no choice but to play in conditions as they are.

No one can control the weather. Nice days can change quickly into poor days, and vice versa. Weather changes and general conditions vary greatly from one part of the country to the next. So what can you do to be ready for a variety of weather conditions?

WHY IS UNDERSTANDING PLAYING CONDITIONS IMPORTANT?

Sometimes you're in the middle of a round, and the rains hit. Or you live in a typically hot climate, and suddenly a cold front moves into your area, and you have to play. Or you usually play in a rather windless climate, and you travel to play in an area like western Texas where there are almost always high, gusty winds blowing. Can you cope with such changes when you play? If not, you'll get less enjoyment out of recreational and competitive play.

Golf requires a degree of flexibility and adaptability. Not everyone who plays the game has the luxury to be ultraselective. Again, as we pointed out in our discussion of sand conditions, *awareness* is important in understanding and adapting to playing conditions. Being aware can save you strokes. Be aware of your normal setup position and ball flight tendencies. Be alert to subsequent changes you need to make to cope with various playing conditions. Know the differences in playing in rainy, wet conditions, compared to dry conditions; or on windy days, compared to calm days. Your swing doesn't change, but your thinking must adapt to the conditions. You learn to cope with, rather than fight, the elements to improve your game.

HOW TO ADAPT TO PLAYING CONDITIONS

Advanced golfers must learn to cope with many types of playing conditions. We will discuss three of these in this section: wind, rain, and temperature extremes. Some players turn adverse conditions into advantages; others allow the conditions to beat them before they start. Let this section help you look for advantages!

Wind

Wind affects both the distance and the direction of ball flight. Light winds are not a problem, but you will notice some effects in winds above 10 to 15 mph.

Wind can blow from any direction. For simplicity, let's put you at the center of your wind compass (see Figure 9.1). Imagine you are preparing to execute your shot. You are standing behind the ball, facing the target, deciding on your plan of action. Wind that comes from your right or left is called "crosswind." Wind that blows toward your face is called "head wind," and wind that blows toward your back is called a "tail wind."

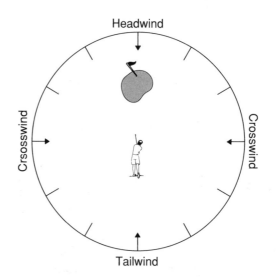

Figure 9.1 Using your wind compass in shot preparation.

You may have observed players on television, or on the courses where you play, throwing grass into the air. They are determining the direction and speed of the wind by watching its effect on the grass. You should also look at the trees or bushes close to your ball position, as well as those near the target area. If you are playing a course with trees lining the fairway, the wind is often blocked. This will tend to give you a false reading of the actual wind conditions that will affect the ball in the air. Look at the flag on the green to get additional information about the wind.

If there is ever a conflict between the wind information you get at the ball and what you observe with the flag or trees closest to the target, go with the target information. The wind will have its greatest effect as the ball begins to slow down (on its descent).

Considerations for Playing in Crosswinds

Crosswinds have the greatest effect on the direction of the ball as it slows down. The ball tends to move off-line in the direction the wind is blowing, so you must make a careful shot selection when hitting to the green. For example, high shots tend to drift more than lower trajectory shots. You may consider playing a pitch and run rather than a lob shot onto the green. If the distance would usually be a full swing with an 8-iron for you, you could choke down on the grip of a 7-iron and make a 4-to-4 swing length—this would produce a lower ball flight while still sending the ball about the same distance as your full swing 8-iron. The distance drills in Step 3 will help you learn to alter trajectory while controlling for distance.

Ball flight curvature is also affected by crosswinds. Curvature in the direction the wind is blowing is accentuated. For example, if you play right-handed and tend to hook the ball, in a right-to-left crosswind your hook will be accentuated (see Figure 9.2). The converse is true for curvature into the wind—your degree of hook would be lessened if the wind is blowing left to right. Note that the degree of drift is an unknown. As you begin to play in wind conditions, you will become more aware of the effects of crosswinds on *your* ball flight.

If your normal ball flight has a slight degree of curvature, you can adjust your alignment to allow for the ball to drift. If the curvature is excessive, the drills provided in Step 2 for controlling ball flight should be practiced with crosswinds in mind. Anytime you can allow for your normal ball flight, use it!

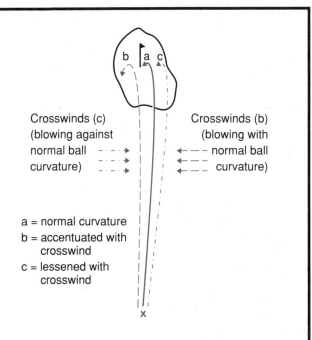

Figure 9.2 Effects of crosswinds on ball curvature: (a) normal curvature, (b) accentuated curvature, (c) lessened curvature.

Considerations for Playing in Head Winds and Tail Winds

Head and tail winds primarily influence the distance the ball travels. Head winds tend to decrease, and tail winds to increase, the distance the ball travels both in the air and rolling on the ground. The amount of increase or decrease in distance depends on wind speed and ball trajectory. Obviously, the higher the wind speed, the greater its effect. A low-trajectory shot is less affected than a high-trajectory shot. A low-trajectory shot is easier to control and more predictable coming in to the green. So the same type shot selections as used in crosswinds could be used here when hitting to the greens. Note that if you are hitting with the wind, you generally aim short of the pin because the ball will roll farther. The opposite is true if you are hitting against the wind (see Figure 9.3, a and b).

If you want to get additional distance from a tail wind, you want to get the ball up into the wind. For example, if you tend to hit a fairly low tee shot with your driver, you may want to tee the ball up a little higher or select a higher lofted wood, such as a 3-wood. The ball will roll more when it lands in a tail wind. Depending on wind speed, it could potentially add 10 or more yards to the distance the ball travels. This makes club selection on all shots more difficult, particularly shots to the green.

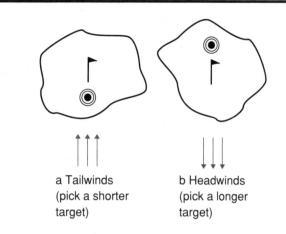

a Tailwinds
(pick a shorter
target)

b Headwinds
(pick a longer
target)

Figure 9.3 Head wind and tail wind target considerations.

A head wind decreases distance in proportion to how high the shot goes and how long it stays in the air. A high shot into the wind looses considerable distance, more than a low shot would. You are usually better off to select a club one to two clubs longer when hitting into the wind. This reduces the tendency to try to swing too hard or fast, which can make you miss your shot. Playing the ball back slightly in your stance will also help to keep the shot lower into the wind. Use the drills in Step 2 on trajectory control to help you practice for these conditions.

Rain

Rain conditions provide their own distinctive challenges. Now you have the umbrella to handle, rainsuits to get into and out of, wet gloves and clubs to hit with, and generally sloppy grass to walk in and hit from. Sounds like fun, doesn't it? Right away you can set your attitude to be successful or unsuccessful. Rain's *inconveniences* can become *distractions*. You can control the distractions, or they can control you!

If rain is forecasted and you're not competing, remember that you have the choice to play or not play. If you choose to play, be ready! Several equipment items are important but optional. A golf umbrella is better than a regular umbrella—it's larger, and provides a convenient space to hook your towels and gloves to keep them dry. Rainsuits help keep you dry and psychologically more comfortable. All-cotton gloves or handkerchiefs tend to provide a better grip than leather gloves when they get wet. The handkerchief can be wrapped around the club grip. Small towels are great for drying grips and clubs.

Light rains create no special problems. They tend to come and go, and light rain is usually absorbed into the ground quickly. Heavy rain or rain that sets in for a time are what create the changes from normal playing conditions. The rain saturates the ground, causing water to pool. This produces areas of standing, or "casual," water. The rules allow a free drop from these areas. Refer to your current *USGA Rules Book* (Rule 25) for the procedures for dropping from areas of casual water.

To play soaked fairways and greens not under casual water, you need to make slight modifications in your setup and shot selection. The greatest swing concern in these wet conditions is hitting heavy or fat shots. These shots can be reduced by moving the ball position back slightly in your stance. This will help you contact the ball first rather than take a divot behind or under the ball.

When the ground is wet, the ball will not roll as much, so your distance will be reduced. To adjust for this, select more club than you would normally hit. For example, where your normal club selection is a 6-iron, select a 5-iron. This will help you focus on maintaining your swing control rather than fighting the conditions.

Your putting will also be affected in rain. As you walk on the green, note its texture. Is it firm or soft? Wet greens are slower than dry greens. Watch the ball as others putt, if you have the opportunity—you can learn about the speed of the green and how much the rain has effected it. Greens with a lot of slope or undulations drain better than flat greens. The speed of these greens or sloped areas will tend not to be as slow as the flatter areas, which hold more water. Before putting, you may want to walk from your ball to the hole, feeling the texture of the green. However, **do not** walk on your putting line or on another player's line, and remember, never feel the green with your hand or you will incur a penalty.

You may need to alter your trap play. Sand that is normally soft and powdery can be made firmer by heavy rains. The ball will come out faster. You will need to adjust your ball position by moving the ball back in your stance to hit less sand.

"Casual water" and "embedded balls" are common during and after rain. Be sure to review the rules for these situations in your *USGA Rule Book* (Rule 25). Knowledge of these rules, as of all rules, can save you strokes.

Rain causes distractions. Acknowledge it. Cope with it. Try to establish a routine—when and where to place the umbrella, dry the grips, put the towel, and so on. This you must do in your own way. But some order will help your composure and turn the distractions into positives.

Warning—Lightning

Lightning has been a real danger to golfers in recent years. Golf clubs, spikes, and anything else metal can attract lightning. **Heed all warnings.** If you are playing in a tournament and you see lightning, you are not required to continue playing. Check with your tournament officials for interpretation and procedures to follow.

Temperature Extremes

Your body has its own internal thermostat. As a result, through the years you have established your own temperature comfort zone, giving you greater tolerance for temperatures that are either hotter or colder than your normal environment. Whether your preference is for hot or cold temperatures, the following considerations will help you prepare for temperature extremes.

Hot Weather

For most people, hot weather is temperatures in and above the high 80s. In dry climates these are tolerable temperatures. However, in humid areas these temperatures can create a mild to tremendous drain on your energy.

There are general guidelines you can follow to cope with high temperatures and high humidity. When given a choice, avoid playing or practicing during the heat of the day (usually between 11 and 3 o'clock). If you decide to practice during this time, allot more time to your short game—it consumes less energy, and it may be easier to concentrate on. Limit your practice time if you're in the direct heat, and avoid sand practice in the heat of the day. The temperatures in sand can easily be 10 or more degrees higher than the surrounding air. Rest and drink cool liquids frequently. Towels and extra gloves are a must, particularly if you perspire. Clubs have been known to fly out of your hands on hot days, so wipe your hands and grips often.

During play, you may find that you fatigue more easily and lose your concentration. This is common. Heat tends to make some people lethargic. Seek the shade whenever possible; keep a damp, cool towel around your neck; drink fluids frequently, but not excessively, remembering that one of the first signs of dehydration is fatigue. If you usually carry your

bag, it may be less fatiguing to pull a cart on extremely hot days. It also helps psychologically to avoid comments and conversations regarding the heat.

Dressing for the heat is also important. Wear light-colored clothing to reduce heat absorption. Choose cotton fabrics over synthetics; cotton is cooler and absorbs perspiration more effectively. Hats are a must, because heat is absorbed through your head—the additional shade provided through a hat, rather than a visor, helps keep you cooler.

Cold Temperatures

Cold temperatures may begin in the 60-degree range for you; this will be determined by your tolerance. Temperatures in this range are tolerable for most players if the sun is out and the day is calm. If it's windy, the windchill can make it too cold for comfort.

Dressing warmly for a walk on a cold day is one thing, but dressing for golf is another. Too much clothing and bulkiness will inhibit your swing. Dress in (thin) layers whenever possible. Thermal underwear and socks are great. Turtlenecks and wool sweaters are good in the cold and help retain body heat. It also helps to wear a layer of cotton under the wool to absorb perspiration. Wear a hat or stocking cap to reduce heat loss through your head, and keep a pair of gloves on whenever you're not swinging. Walking versus riding helps to generate more body heat.

Be sure to warm up before you play. Your muscles take longer to loosen up in cold weather. You don't have to hit balls in your warm-up. Make 20 or so practice swings, starting slowly and working up to your normal swing speed. Your swing will tend not to be as free in cold weather, because of the extra clothing. Use more club and try not to overpower your shots.

PLAYING CONDITIONS AWARENESS

Awareness of how weather conditions affect your play is critical to becoming a better player. Until you are very aware of your skills, you should keep a record of various conditions, such as rain, wind, cold, and heat, and the accommodations you must make for each. Then you must assess your adaptability to the conditions and describe your strengths or weaknesses in adapting.

Keeping a record or using the checklist in Figure 9.4 will make you accountable for your improvement. It is easy to blame poor play and high scores on the weather and resulting playing conditions. But if you chart your play, you will become more conscious of the areas to improve and realize that you are in control of your play.

Learning to cope with various playing conditions is important in becoming a good player.

The sun does not always shine on the golf course. Figure 9.4 provides a brief review to raise your awareness of playing conditions, their effects, and the adaptations you need to make for them. Read the description of the playing condition, then correctly determine the effects and the adaptations needed.

Figure 9.4 Keys to Success: Playing Conditions Awareness Checklist

Playing condition	Effect	Adaptation
Wind		
Head wind	____ Decreases distance	____ Club selection (need more club)
Tail wind	____ Increases distance	____ Club selection (need less club)
Crosswind	____ Direction/distance	____ Alignment
		____ Club selection
Rain	____ Distance	____ Ball position
		____ Club selection
	____ Distraction	____ Equipment
		____ Routine
Heat	____ Fatigue	____ Clothing
	____ Discomfort	____ Limit practice/play
		____ Drink liquids
		____ Seek shade
		____ Moist towels
		____ Club selection
Cold	____ Discomfort	____ Layer clothing
		____ Cover head
		____ Avoid carts
	____ Decreases distance	____ Club selection
		____ Restricted swings

Detecting Playing Condition Errors

Awareness is a key in detecting playing condition errors. Learning to cope with a variety of weather conditions comes through experience. The following suggestions for playing and adjusting to situations will help you cognitively understand the impact of weather on your golf skills. However, actual experience with the conditions will provide the trial and error necessary for you to make these a part of your game.

ERROR ⃠	CORRECTION
1. During play in crosswinds, you consistently miss the green to the right.	1. Check your alignment. Review Figure 9.1 for a visual picture of playing in crosswinds.
2. The ball goes on-line to the target, but in crosswinds the curvature is accentuated and the green is missed to the left.	2a. Practice Drill 1 (see Figure 9.2) to allow for your natural curvature. 2b. Review the drills in Step 2 for controlling curvature.
3. When playing in head winds, you hit short of target.	3. Take one or two clubs more to allow for distance lost in the wind.
4. High pitch shots are difficult to control in head and tail winds.	4. Hit a pitch and run shot for control. A high shot is difficult to predict and is not very effective in the wind.
5. You commonly hit fat shots (hitting the ground before the ball) in the rain.	5. Move the ball position back slightly in your stance.
6. It takes you five or six holes to loosen up in cold weather.	6. Be sure to warm up by hitting balls or making practice swings before playing.
7. High humidity drains your energy and results in poor play.	7. Dress appropriately and keep a cool towel around your neck. Seek shade and drink cool fluids frequently. Use longer clubs on shots to the green.

Playing Condition Drills

Practicing in a variety of playing conditions is important for acclimating yourself and your swing adaptations for those conditions. Temperature extremes and wind are fairly easy to practice in. However, take caution in rain, given the many lightning strikes in recent years. Check the forecast to be sure no storms are in the area.

Consider the following on-course situations and respond to the questions. See answers for Drills 1-4 at the end of this step.

1. Wind Drill

Pretend you are playing in a right-to-left crosswind, with gusts up to 15 mph. Your normal ball flight is left to right. You are hitting a 5-iron to the green from the left side of the fairway.

Success Goal = Shade the following diagram, indicating your target area for your 5-iron

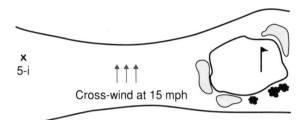

5-i

Cross-wind at 15 mph

Your Score = Target area correctly defined

2. Rain Drill

Imagine you are playing in a steady rain. The course is saturated, but playable. You have hit numerous shots "fat." What adjustments do you need to make to improve your ball contact?

Success Goal = Identifying the adjustments needed because of rain

Your Score = Correctly identifying the adjustments you can make that will reduce the effect of the rain

3. Heat Drill

Imagine that the temperature is 95 degrees. You are carrying your bag and feeling very tired. What can you do to reduce the effect of the heat?

Success Goal = Identifying the adjustments you should make due to the heat

Your Score = Correctly identifying the adjustments you can make that will reduce the effect of the heat

4. Cold Drill

Imagine that north winds are blowing at gusts up to 20 mph. The temperature is 65 degrees with a windchill of 45 degrees. You are preparing to play. What adaptations should you consider for this condition?

Success Goal = Specifying the adjustments you should make due to the cold and wind

Your Score = Correctly identify the adjustments needed to play in the cold and wind

5. Record Playing Conditions

Players often blame weather conditions for poor play, never taking time to evaluate why or how the weather really affected their play. The chart in Figure 9.5 will help you reflect on weather conditions over time. Use it to identify your abilities to adapt and your areas of improvement.

Success Goal =

    a. Chart 10 rounds of variable playing conditions

    b. Review your rounds, noting areas needing improvement

    c. Plan strategies for practicing and playing in those conditions

Your Score =

    a. (#) ____ rounds played and recorded

    b. (#) ____ weaknesses identified

    c. (#) ____ practice sessions implementing planned strategies

| Date | Score | Course | Weather conditions | | | | | Playing conditions description | Adaptability Areas adapted/need to improve | Rating 5/excellent - 1/poor |
			Sun	Rain	Cold/Temp.	Hot/Temp.	Wind/mph.			
4/16	81	Cog Hill			✓ / 52	/	✓ / 20	Cold and windy with wet ground	Dressed in layers and walked. Played crosswinds w/short irons.	2
					/	/	/			
					/	/	/			
					/	/	/			
					/	/	/			
					/	/	/			
					/	/	/			
					/	/	/			
					/	/	/			
					/	/	/			
					/	/	/			
					/	/	/			
					/	/	/			

Figure 9.5 Chart for recording playing conditions.

Playing Conditions
Keys to Success Checklist

Awareness of how weather conditions affect your play is critical in becoming a better player. The checklist in Figure 9.4 allows you to check your understanding of various conditions, such as rain, wind, heat, and cold. You should also keep track of your ability to play in such conditions, and be aware of your strengths or weaknesses in adapting. If you monitor your play, you will become more conscious of the areas to improve and realize that you are in control of your play.

Answers to Step 9 Drills

Wind Drill (#1)

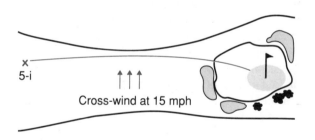

Rain Drill (#2)

To adjust for "fat" shots made in the rain, you can move the ball position back in your stance to avoid hitting too much ground before the ball. Make practice swings to determine the low point of your arc and the desired ball position.

Heat Drill (#3)

To help thermoregulate, you should wear a hat and light-colored clothes. It is also helpful to wear a wet towel around your neck and drink a few sips of cool water before each hole.

If the weather is also dry, anticipate longer rolls of your ball and firmer greens.

Cold Drill (#4)

1. Adaptations for cold: Wear layers of clothing to insulate your body, plus gloves and hat.
2. Adaptations for wind: Before hitting each shot, determine the relationship of the wind to your target direction. Make the following adjustments, depending on wind direction.

   • Hitting into the wind: Hit a lower shot; choke down on the grip of a larger club or move the ball slightly back in your stance, away from the target.
   • Hitting with the wind: Use the wind to your advantage by hitting a higher club and adjusting for the increased distance.
   • Hitting with crosswind: Remember that ball flight curvature will be exaggerated with the wind and moderated (made less) if curving into the wind.

Step 10 Influences of Course Design on Course Management

Once you have learned all of the other skills of golf, it is important to learn how to "play" the course. Each golf course layout is unique and designed to present special challenges to the golfer. Learning to assess the various aspects of each golf hole is critical in becoming a proficient golfer.

WHY IS COURSE MANAGEMENT IMPORTANT?

Golf course architects generally attempt to provide both aesthetically pleasing and challenging course layouts. To play your best golf, you must match your strengths with the weaknesses of each golf hole. Holes are designed to draw your attention to the "trouble," or "strengths," of the hole, but you must direct your shots to the safest locations to maximize your chances for a low score. Understanding the strengths and weaknesses of each hole will help you plan each shot to produce the best results.

A hole's strengths are the elements that add challenge to each shot—the sand traps, water hazards, trees, bushes, fairway bunkers, slope of the green, pin placement, and so on. Notice that even their names imply threats (e.g., "hazards," "traps"). If you play into these strengths, your score will reflect the trouble. On the other hand, the weaknesses of a hole are the landing areas and safe locations where you would like to play your shots. If you play into these weaknesses, your score will reflect your strengths.

LEARNING TO MANAGE A ROUND OF GOLF

Each time you play a round of golf, you should begin by analyzing the entire layout of the course. Get a copy of the scorecard and familiarize yourself with the location of each hole, the shape of the holes (straight, dogleg, etc.), the relative size of the greens, traps, and water. Begin with this global picture of the course you are about to play. Some courses have booklets with the layout of each hole, yardage markers to indicate the distances from various points to the green, and often descriptions of the best way to play the hole.

Each hole should also be analyzed for its strengths and weaknesses. Notice the hole's par, and determine where your first shot should land and how you will enter the green. To do this, you must begin with a broad look at the hole itself. Identify the hole's strengths (traps, vegetation, out of bounds [OB], water, etc.), and then focus on the weaknesses, or desired landing areas. Once you know your options, you can match the weaknesses of the hole with the strengths of your game. If you are an accurate and "big" hitter, you can afford to go for the longer, more difficult shots. If you are a moderately long hitter, you may need to plan both your first and second shots *at once*.

To focus your attention for the round, it is often helpful to use the scorecards courses provide to plan out the shots you *expect* on each hole. What are the demand characteristics of the hole, and how will you match your strengths to capitalize on the design of this particular hole. These first two phases of analyzing a hole require that you begin with a broad, external focus of attention, and then match the information gained to your own skills as a golfer (using a broad, internal focus). The third phase is to actually survey the shot at hand (having a narrow, external focus). Determine the lie of the ball, the desired trajectory, and the actual distance to the desired landing area. It is easy to remember this third phase by the acronym *LTD*:

- Lie
- Trajectory
- Distance

The fourth phase is to choose the shot you will attempt (both the club and the type of swing), matching your particular skills with the demands of this particular situation (using a narrow, internal focus). And lastly, you must concentrate on executing the planned shot (using a narrow, external, target-oriented focus). This sequence is outlined in Table 10.1.

Table 10.1 Attentional Demands in Golf

Attentional demands	Sequence for analyzing a hole
1. Broad external focus	Select route
2. Broad internal focus	Consider skills
3. Narrow external focus	Use LTD method (consider lie, trajectory, and distance
4. Narrow internal focus	Select club and motion
5. Narrow external focus	Think target, and trust

Using the LTD method is essential to successful course management. If the lie of the ball is good, you have the maximum number of alternatives. But a poor lie limits both the trajectory and the distance you can get from the ball. For this reason, never select a club before you have investigated the ball's lie. When a ball is not sitting up on grass (e.g., it's in a divot or on hard, bare dirt), your options are reduced. Your second consideration is trajectory. If you must loft the ball to avoid a hazard or vegetation, or land without much roll, you must determine that before you consider what club will get you the desired distance (the last of the three considerations). LTD will determine, for example, which variation of the pitch shot you will use (as described in Step 4).

One of the most difficult aspects of course management is to evaluate each shot you make. It is essential that you be able to differentiate between a shot that was poorly executed, but well planned, and a poor plan based on limited information.

It is also important to be able to decide when you are really in trouble and when you can afford to gamble. For example, if you hit a ball into the rough, and it comes to rest behind a tree, when should you hit it forward and when should you simply lag into the fairway to be in a better position for the next shot? These types of decisions distinguish the dedicated golfer. It is critical to know when you are in over your head, and take the safe way out.

Proficient golfers effectively manage their "game plan" by matching their strengths to the weaknesses of each hole on the course. They determine a route to the hole and consider the LTD method for each shot. If their first shot is executed just as planned, they are ready to check the LTD for the second shot and proceed. On the other hand, if the first shot was not exactly as planned, they are flexible and plan a new route to the hole. This method of analyzing the strengths and weaknesses of each hole is summarized in Figure 10.1.

Figure 10.1 Keys to Success: Course Management

Preparation Phase

1. Survey the entire layout of the golf course ____ (Notice the number and location of doglegs, par 5s, large bodies of water, and so forth.)

2. Identify the general relationships of each hole to each other hole ____

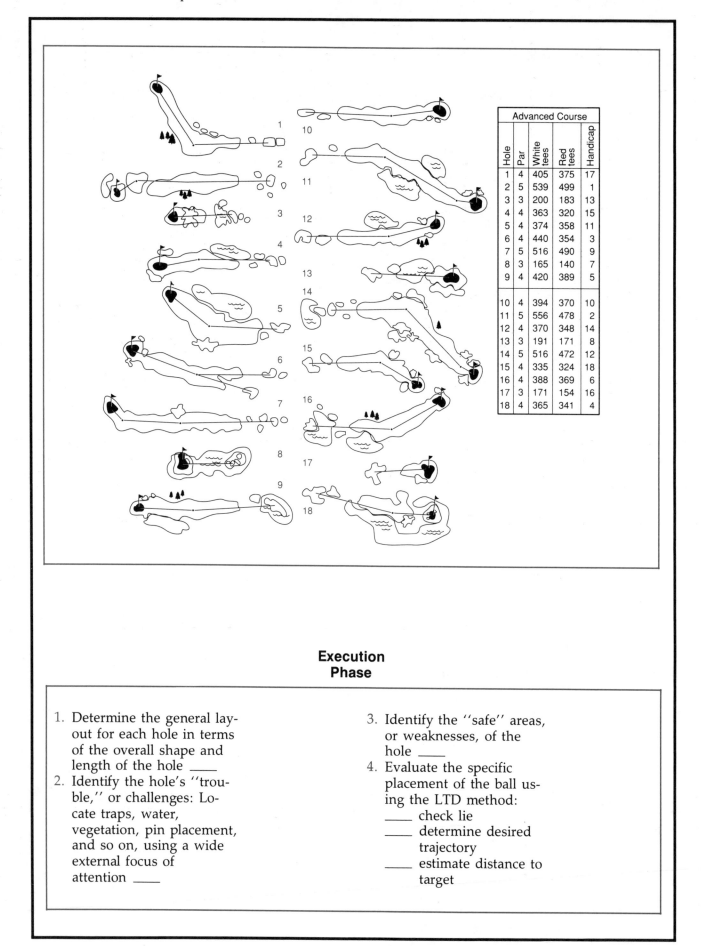

	Advanced Course			
Hole	Par	White tees	Red tees	Handicap
1	4	405	375	17
2	5	539	499	1
3	3	200	183	13
4	4	363	320	15
5	4	374	358	11
6	4	440	354	3
7	5	516	490	9
8	3	165	140	7
9	4	420	389	5
10	4	394	370	10
11	5	556	478	2
12	4	370	348	14
13	3	191	171	8
14	5	516	472	12
15	4	335	324	18
16	4	388	369	6
17	3	171	154	16
18	4	365	341	4

Execution Phase

1. Determine the general layout for each hole in terms of the overall shape and length of the hole ____
2. Identify the hole's "trouble," or challenges: Locate traps, water, vegetation, pin placement, and so on, using a wide external focus of attention ____
3. Identify the "safe" areas, or weaknesses, of the hole ____
4. Evaluate the specific placement of the ball using the LTD method:
   ____ check lie
   ____ determine desired trajectory
   ____ estimate distance to target

5. Consider your own strengths as a golfer: What kind of club do I want to hit given this LTD information? Do I want to use a fairway wood or an iron for my second shot? Which side of the green is the best to approach from? ____

6. Match your strengths with the weaknesses of the hole. Focus on the target ____

Follow-Through Phase

Ask yourself two questions after each shot:

1. "Did I make the right decision?"

   a. After hitting the shot, determine if you made the correct decision about where to aim, and what club to hit ____

   b. If not, consider what you should have planned to do, so you will make a better decision the next time a similar situation arises ____

2. "Did I execute what I had planned to do?" ____

   a. Determine if you executed the shot you had planned ____

   b. If not, consider how you should have executed the shot. It is sometimes helpful to take a practice swing after a poor shot to establish the desirable image and memory ____

Detecting Errors in Course Management

Most course management errors arise from either not taking time to gain all the information you need to make a good plan, or not trusting yourself to carry out the plan and therefore not executing a good swing. The second set of errors generally results when you focus your attention on the hole's "strengths," or trouble spots, rather than focusing on the hole's weaknesses and your desired behaviors.

ERROR

CORRECTION

1. Failing to take into account the roll of the ball on dry grass.

2. Allowing anxiety to build over the presence of water.

3. Failing to notice pin placement.

4. Hitting a low-percentage shot when a safer one is available.

5. Ball was underhit because it was in a divot.

1. Be sure to examine the greens and fairways before playing.

2. Focus attention on the ''safe'' or desirable landing areas.

3. Always begin by focusing on the desired endpoint—the hole with the pin in it.

4. Intermediate players should generally be conservative in the shots they attempt (i.e., play the percentages with the safer shot).

5. Be sure to use the LTD method: first consider the lie of the ball, then the desired trajectory, and finally the desired distance.

Course Management Drills

1. Course Management Drill

Survey the sample diagram of an 18-hole course. Study the design, and then circle or color in all the trouble spots on each hole (use red for the hole's strengths). Then locate the safe areas or weaknesses of the course, and shade them in differently.

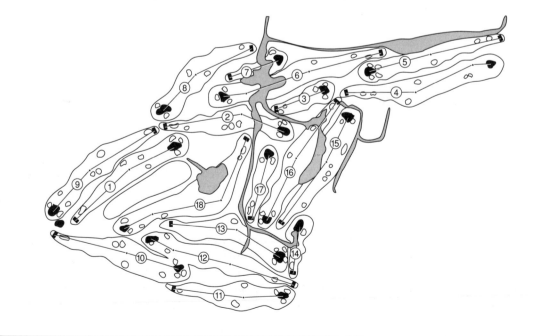

Success Goal = Identify at least 3 strengths and 3 weaknesses for each hole

Your Score = [Compare your answers with those at the end of this step]

(#) _____ of strengths identified (3 per hole = 54)

(#) _____ of weaknesses identified (3 per hole = 54)

2. Create 9 Holes Drill

Draw 9 golf holes, each one on a separate sheet of paper. Be creative, adding both strengths and weaknesses to each hole. Establish a par and hole distance for each hole. Then play each hole as you would on the course, by drawing each shot on the diagram.

Success Goal = Identify at least 3 strengths and 3 weaknesses for each hole

Your Score =

a. (#) _____ of strengths identified (3 per hole = 27)

b. (#) _____ of weaknesses identified (3 per hole = 27)

3. Play a Round in Your Head

While standing on the practice tee, imagine that you are playing a round of golf. Draw a diagram of your home course in your head. For each shot, identify a target on the driving range and the club you will use. (Be sure to vary the LTD: lie, trajectory, and distance.) Then actually hit each shot as planned.

Success Goal = To be able to actually picture an entire 18 holes and play against the course in your imagination (scores here indicate the number of shots executed, even if not hit as imagined)

Your Score =

Hole number	Number shots imagined and hit	Hole number	Number shots imagined and hit
1	_____	10	_____
2	_____	11	_____
3	_____	12	_____
4	_____	13	_____
5	_____	14	_____
6	_____	15	_____
7	_____	16	_____
8	_____	17	_____
9	_____	18	_____

4. Scorecard Travel Plans Drill

Just before you play a round at a local golf course, plot out your plan for each hole on the scorecard they provide—either for all 18 holes at the start, or just before each new hole. Be sure to note the strengths and weaknesses of each hole first, as shown here.

Success Goal = Diagram both the desired and the actual route for each shot on the scorecard; be sure to use your realistic distances and not necessarily the route that would be required for a par on each hole

Your Score =

    a. (#) ____ holes drawn as you would actually play them

    b. (✓) ____ actually draw in the shots you hit; when you are finished compare the desired strategy with what actually happened

5. Partner Designed Shots

With a partner, take turns describing a hole and then watching your partner actually play the hole from the driving range. Partners should describe strengths and weaknesses of the hole, and the person hitting should identify the intended strategy before hitting. Imagine playing out that hole, and then change roles. Repeat 5 times.

Success Goal =

    a. Describe 5 holes for your partner to play from the driving range

    b. Play 5 holes your partner has described

Your Score =

    a. (#) ____ holes described for partner

    b. (#) ____ holes played according to the strategy designed for the hole (the partner determines whether the player executed the hole as planned)

Course Management
Keys to Success Checklist

Being able to strike the ball well will not in itself make you a good golfer. You must be able to plan your shots by analyzing the characteristics of each hole. Effective golfers use a systematic approach to reviewing the entire course layout, the uniqueness of each hole, and the particular requirements of each shot. Use the checklist in Figure 10.1 to evaluate your ability to systematically manage a round of golf.

Answer to Drill 1

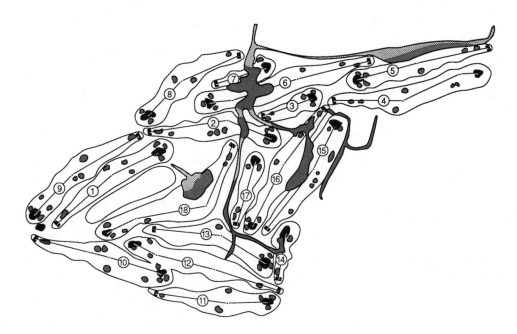

Note: Open areas indicated hole weaknesses.

Step 11 Developing Confidence: The Power of Positive Thinking

Being self-confident is a key to successful golf. Self-confidence is a belief or trust in yourself and feeling sure that you will be able to perform the skills required. To be self-confident, you must have developed the skills to be competent as a golfer—your confidence grows from your competence. There's no point in trying to fool yourself if your head and heart know you haven't practiced a particular shot. But if you have put in the time to train your muscles, you should be able to trust them.

Self-confidence involves a certain degree of arrogance, because of the certainty you feel about your ability to perform. The key is to be very cocky inside, but not talk about it too much. Most people don't like overly confident individuals, so we learn to be gracious winners and not talk about how good we think we are. However, to be a great golfer, you must know that you are good!

WHY IS SELF-CONFIDENCE IMPORTANT?

To be self-confident, you must think confidently, feel confident, and act confident. It doesn't do any good to think you are a great putter, if every time you have a 3-foot putt, you let your anxious feelings produce an uneven stroke. Before each putt, you must think you are going to make it and then put a stroke on the ball that will allow you to make it.

One of the most dangerous things golfers can do is question their ability to hit a certain shot. If you have doubts about hitting a 5-iron, you will likely overcerebrate about it. If you try to remember everything you should do (''Keep your eye on the ball, pivot to the rear, keep your left arm extended, release at the ball, follow through,'' etc.), there is no way you can really execute the shot. You are likely to suffer from ''paralysis by analysis.'' Instead you must trust yourself to hit the shot, and get your mind out of the way of your swing.

Another example of a devastating effect of not trusting yourself is to stand over the ball wondering if you have selected the right club. If that

happens to you, you should recognize it as a self-doubting thought, back away from the shot, and say a positive statement to yourself. Then start the shot all over, from the beginning of your preshot routine.

HOW TO BUILD SELF-CONFIDENCE

The most important thing you can do to build self-confidence is to know yourself and be able to make realistic decisions about what you can do. An important strategy is to assess your skills as they are today, then set realistic *goals*, and then give yourself feedback about your skills. By practicing with specific goals in mind, you will be able to judge your competence and develop self-confidence.

In combination with goal setting, it is critical that you complement your skills with the thoughts you think. Literally, you must be your own best cheerleader. It has been said that ''winners think about what they *want* to happen; losers think about what they fear will happen.'' For example, if you are standing on a par 3 that requires a 150-yard drive over water, do you think about landing in the water or about landing on that big green? The idea of course management is to think about the target. You should think about the *desired target*, and believe that you can get there!

HOW TO USE POSITIVE SELF-TALK TO IMPROVE SELF-CONFIDENCE

The way you talk to yourself directly reflects how you feel about yourself and how you act. Your mind is like a complex computer that processes information that is only as good as the data that is fed into it. If negative thoughts and feelings are the ones you feed your computer, then you will likely find yourself with a poor self-concept and a swing that matches it. In contrast, if you feed yourself thoughts and feelings that are based on your competence, your self-confidence will be elevated.

To improve your positive, self-enhancing talk, pay attention to what you are saying to yourself. All people talk to themselves; but winners say more positive things than losers. That does not mean that winners never criticize themselves or doubt a decision they have made. But when winners say negative things to themselves, they replace the negative statements with positive ones before trying to hit a shot.

Substitute Positive for Negative Thoughts

One of the most important techniques for positive thinking is to get rid of negative thoughts. If your head is full of negative things, it's like a garbage can full of trash. After a while it begins to stink, and so will your game. You must get that garbage out in order to clean the air. Begin this process by identifying any negative thought you might have. For example, if you are about to tee off on a hole where you hit the ball out of bounds during the last round, you may be thinking, "I hate this hole, I always hit the ball OB left." That negative thought is not only not true (you only did it the last time), it will negatively affect your swing. You must replace that thought with a good one, such as "I know I can hit this driver when I focus on my preshot routine and then let it go." This new, replacement thought will direct your thinking without trying to steer your club.

When you have a negative thought, you must interrupt it and replace it with a positive one. It is often good to literally interrupt it with an action, such as hitting the side of your hip, tapping the sole of your shoe, or just saying "Stop." Take a deep breath, and exhale deeply to let go of that thought. Then replace it with a positive statement. The following four-part process will help you stop negative, self-defeating thoughts and replace them with self-enhancing thoughts.

1. Recognize negative thought.
2. Interrupt negative thought.
3. Take a deep breath and let it go.
4. Replace the negative thought with a positive statement.

Affirmations

Positive statements, or *affirmations*, can also be used to enhance your self-confidence. Just saying "I feel good about myself because I am in control of my behavior" can have a wonderful impact. Each positive affirmation is recorded in your memory, so that as long as there are more positives than negatives, you will feel good about yourself. The higher the percentage of positives, the better. Try statements like these:

- I am a winner because I am in charge.
- I am a great putter.
- I love to hit a chip shot.
- I am confident when I get around the green.
- I am committed to being a better golfer.
- I can focus my attention in any environment.
- Attitude is a decision, and I've decided to be a winner.
- I always repeat the good but replace the bad.

Notice that these are statements about what exists. Not hopes such as "I want to be . . ." or "I wish I were . . . ." The last statement is perhaps the most important one: "Repeat the good, but replace the bad." Whenever you have a bad or negative thought, replace it with a positive one. Similarly if you have a great shot, take a minute to savor it and feel it (repeat it in your mind). If your shot is not great, replace it with a good practice swing or the image of one in your mind. When you hit a great shot, say something good about your behavior (e.g., "I really used my preshot routine" or "I let go, and it was a great swing").

There are also some thoughts that are not really "negative" but are definitely counterproductive. For example, recognizing that you can control only the shot you are about to make is critical. It does no good to think about the last hole ("Oh, if I just hadn't gone OB, I'd be even with par right now") or future shots ("All I need is to stay even on the next three holes, and I can win this"). Thinking about the past or future definitely disrupts your ability to concentrate on the present. The only shot that matters is this one, so stay in the present.

Similarly, thinking about the people around you is also not productive. It is fine to chat between shots or to think about the slow players in front of you while you walk down the fairway. But when it is time to hit, you must put those thoughts out of your mind. Thoughts about the weather or course conditions are also elements you can't control, so why let them interfere with your swing? You must consider such things as a crosswind when you plan your shot, but you should not be thinking about it as you hit your shot.

Understanding and using the basic phases of thought stoppage and positive thinking will help you become a better golfer. These phases are outlined in Figure 11.1.

Figure 11.1 Keys to Success:
Positive Thinking

Preparation Phase

"I wonder if I'm lined up for this putt?"

1. Recognize a negative thought ____

a

Execution Phase

"STOP! I better start my putting routine all over–"

"I've used my routine, and I'm ready to hit a great putt."

b   c   d

1. Interrupt the negative thought ____
2. Take a deep breath ____
3. Exhale deeply to expel ("let go of") the negative thought ____

4. Make a positive statement to replace the negative thought ____

Follow-Up
Phase

1. After a shot, say something positive about your behavior ____

2. "Repeat the good, replace the bad" ____

Detecting Errors in Self-Talk

It is sometimes difficult to recognize negative patterns of thinking, because no one can see them. You must be honest with yourself in identifying what you tend to think and finding ways to replace any self-defeating thoughts with self-enhancing ones. It is all right to have a critical thought, but it is never effective to try to hit the ball while you're thinking one. Always replace negative thoughts with positive ones that can direct your behavior, before you start your preshot routine or try to hit a ball.

ERROR 🚫

CORRECTION

ERROR	CORRECTION
1. Thinking about past shots while trying to hit the present one.	1. Use the past to help *plan* the present, but do not dwell on the past. Use thought stoppage.
2. Focusing on the strengths of a hole (trouble spots) rather than the weaknesses (safe areas).	2. Focus on the desired target, not the "dangers." Identify desired landing areas before planning the shot.
3. Being concerned about a particular club ("I can't ever seem to hit my 3-iron").	3. Either practice until you can honestly say "I know I can hit ____ ; I've hit it well all week in practice," or say "This is a great chance to try the club I've been working on," or choose another club until you can practice that one. Use thought stoppage to redirect thinking.
4. Worrying about what will happen after golf (e.g., the 3:00 appointment; the "to do" list).	4. Redirect thoughts to this shot. Stay in the "present tense."
5. Thinking about future shots ("If I can just stay out of trouble on the next three holes, it will be my best round ever").	5. Use thought stoppage. Thinking about the future only distracts from the present. Beware that "what-ifs" don't become "whiffs."

Confidence Building and Positive Thinking Drills

1. Identifying Counterproductive Thoughts

Make a list of some of the typical negative or counterproductive thoughts you have during a round of golf or on the practice tee. Take a tablet of paper or a small tape recorder with you and record any thoughts that are not positive or that distract you.

Success Goal = A list of at least 20 thoughts that could be changed to be better or more positive

Negative thoughts (Drill 1)	Positive replacement thoughts (Drill 2)
1. _____	1. _____
2. _____	2. _____
3. _____	3. _____
4. _____	4. _____
5. _____	5. _____
6. _____	6. _____
7. _____	7. _____
8. _____	8. _____
9. _____	9. _____
10. _____	10. _____
11. _____	11. _____
12. _____	12. _____
13. _____	13. _____
14. _____	14. _____
15. _____	15. _____
16. _____	16. _____
17. _____	17. _____
18. _____	18. _____
19. _____	19. _____
20. _____	20. _____

Your Score = (#) _____ of statements recorded in left-hand column

2. Replacement Drill

For each negative thought identified in Drill 1, write a replacement statement in the right-hand column that will be positive and self-enhancing. Make a column list adjacent to each of the negative thoughts (from Drill 1). The positive replacement thoughts should be about the same topic, but stated in a positive, self-enhancing way.

Negative thought	Positive replacement thought
Example A:	
I have to hit over water; I'll use one of my old balls in case I dunk one.	That water is lovely; I'll land on the upper portion of the green where it is wide open.
Example B:	
I can't ever hit out of this long grass. How could I have pushed that last shot so badly!	I've been practicing this shot by really staying down and following through on the shot. I can hit this!

Success Goal = A list of at least 20 positive replacement thoughts, one for each of the negative thoughts identified for Drill 1

Your Score = (#) _____ replacement statements that directly counter the self-defeating thoughts from Drill 1

3. Affirmation Drill

Make a list of 10 positive affirmations about yourself. Print each one on a separate notecard. Each day put a different one in your room, locker, or car and another one in the pocket of your golf bag. Read the cards at least three times each day.

Success Goal = 10 affirmations about your golf skills or ability to control your thoughts and behaviors

Your Score = (#) _____ affirmations written on notecards (record the affirmations here)

1. _____
   _____

2. _____
   _____

3. _____
   _____

4. _____
   _____

5. _____
   _____

6. _____

_____

7. _____

_____

8. _____

_____

9. _____

_____

10. _____

_____

4. Affirmation Practice Drill

Take your list of affirmations with you and read each affirmation at least three times per day for the next 7 days.

Success Goal = Read each affirmation at least 3 times per day for the next 7 days.

Your Score = Number of repetitions per day

(#) _____ times read on Day 1

(#) _____ times read on Day 2

(#) _____ times read on Day 3

(#) _____ times read on Day 4

(#) _____ times read on Day 5

(#) _____ times read on Day 6

(#) _____ times read on Day 7

5. Thought Stoppage on the Course Drill

It is important to practice the strategy of replacing negative thoughts, but it is even more important to use the strategy on the course. Play three holes of golf, and keep track of every nonpositive thought you have. Actively replace each with a positive thought.

Success Goal = Play 3 holes of golf and write down each negative thought you have; also indicate the positive thought you substituted for the negative one (alternative: use a tape recorder or dictaphone)

Your Score = List of negative thoughts and positive replacements for 3 holes

Hole number	Negative thoughts	Positive replacement thoughts
1	_____	_____
	_____	_____
2	_____	_____
	_____	_____
3	_____	_____
	_____	_____

Confidence Building and Positive Thinking Keys to Success Checklist

Positive thinking is a key to self-confidence. Unlike physical skills, it is a mental skill that can be observed only by you. You must be aware of what you think and say to yourself when you practice and play. Ask yourself if you are thinking about your skills or if you are doubting yourself. Remember: "Winners think about what they *want to happen*; losers think about what they fear might happen." You must use your thoughts to direct your attention and behavior. Use the checklist in Figure 11.1 to evaluate your ability to control your thinking.

Step 12 Imagery for Enhanced Performance

There are two ways to practice most golf skills: physical practice and mental practice. By learning to use imagery to improve your golf, not only will you double your practice time, but you will be able to practice before every shot.

Most good golfers use imagery to rehearse their shots. You may have seen the pros close their eyes to imagine a beautiful swing or just stand momentarily as if preoccupied by a thought. This technique of imagining a shot before actually taking it allows you to check your strategy and essentially have a "mulligan" on every shot. To use imagery you must be able to key into all of your senses: seeing, hearing, feeling, touching, tasting, and so on. If you can relax and use those stored images, you will become a much improved golfer.

WHY IS IMAGERY IMPORTANT?

Every shot in golf is slightly different from the last shot, yet similar in that the same muscles and emotions may be used. It is therefore important to be aware of our bodies before we ever hit a shot. Imagery allows you to detect current levels of tension and plan by capitalizing on past experience.

Close your eyes and imagine your favorite food. If you are thinking about a big juicy hamburger with onions and french fries, you may be able to smell it, see it, feel the texture of the meat and the bun and the fries, feel your mouth and throat chew and swallow, and so forth. You can probably imagine in many different senses. Similarly, if you imagine putting a 15-foot uphill putt, you may be able to see the line of the putt, feel the putter in your hands, sense the smooth stroke, and hear the ball hit squarely in the cup. Each of these sensory experiences will reinforce your skill in putting.

Imagery can also be used to practice a new skill. Imagine that you are trying to learn to fade the ball. Watch a good golfer do it, or observe it on videotape or TV. Then imagine your own body executing that shot. Sense the different feelings in your hands as the clubhead slides inside the ball. Think about the different flights of the ball as it curves through the air.

Self-confidence can also be enhanced by imagery of your own golf skills. If you can see yourself hit that 5-iron over the water and land near the pin, you will be better able to execute the shot. Can you picture yourself hitting each of the clubs in your bag?

HOW TO IMAGINE GOLF SHOTS

Using imagery to help your golf is as natural as sleeping every night. When you dream, you sometimes have very realistic thoughts and images. Have you ever awakened and wondered if you really had that conversation with someone or if you really failed that test or stepped off that wall? Dreams are sometimes so realistic that it is hard to tell them from reality. The vividness of dreams can be used to help your golf game through the use of imagery. If you think hard enough about a particular shot, your muscles and all other senses will respond. The key is to use those responses to help you prepare to actually execute the shot.

The first step in using imagery is to be relaxed so that you can "tune in" to all of your senses. The "take a deep breath" technique discussed in Step 11 is a good way to help you focus on the images in your mind. For example, on a par 4 hole with a great landing area approximately 220 yards out, can you imagine the feel of your drive? The way the ball looks in the air? How the club feels as it accelerates and makes contact with the ball? The sound of a nice solid hit?

Every golfer has the capacity to imagine shots. Not everyone conjures up a visual image. For some it is a feeling in the muscles (kinesthetic imagery), for others it is the sound of the club hitting the ball (auditory imagery), and for others it is the visual image of the ball sailing through the air. If you can remember and repeat any of these images, you can use them to help you be a better golfer. It does not matter if you "see the shot" or "feel the swing." The important thing is that you have been able to focus your attention on the memory (image) of previously executed shots. If someone asks you to imagine hitting a perfect drive off the tee, would you feel it, see it, or hear it? Any one of those sensations will help, and being able to imagine in two or more sensory modalities will benefit you all the more.

One of the best ways to tune in to your specific mode of imagination is to reflect on a great shot. The next time you are on the practice tee or course and hit a really great shot, take a moment and "relive" that shot. Do an "instant replay" in your mind. When you think about that great shot, do you see it, feel it, hear it, or what? The best way to discover your primary mode of imagination is to do it (imagine). Remember the last dream you had? Did you wake up shaking or breathing hard, or did you have a vivid visual image? Your mind has a hard time separating dreams from reality. Both excite your muscles and activate your brain, and both can be used to build your confidence.

As part of each preshot routine, take a moment to imagine the shot you are about to hit. If you are a visualizer, imagine the flight of the ball, and "see" the ball land at the desired target. If you imagine in terms of muscle memory or kinesthesis, "feel" the swing before you actually produce it. Can you imagine actually hearing the clubhead hit the ball? In this way, you have a practice shot, or mulligan, for each shot.

It is important to remember that your imagery should always be about the desired shot. Some golfers accidentally doubt their abilities and may inadvertently be affected by a negative image. For example, imagine playing a par 5 hole with a wide stream cutting across the fairway at about 180 yards out. You must decide whether to drive over the water hazard or lag up short of it. Let's say you decide to "go for it" but have a little doubt in the back of your mind. You may even accidentally imagine your ball landing in the water (or you might even take out a "water ball" as some nonconfident golfers do!). These negative images send signals to your body that end up focusing you on the water. Instead you want to focus on the desired landing areas and the active choice you have made to drive over the water. Remember, "winners see what they want to happen; losers see what they fear might happen."

Imagining the best that you can be is the key to the successful use of imagery in golf. Your images will be most vivid about recent shots. If you hit a great drive on the last hole, you should be able to replay that feeling before the next drive. By replaying the good feelings, you will increase your chance of hitting another good shot. A parallel principle would be to avoid remembering bad shots by replacing their image with a more positive image. Some professional golfers have learned to replace the image of a bad shot by taking another practice swing before leaving the location of the weak or poor shot. That is, after a good shot, immediately replay it as you walk to the next shot; but if you happen to hit a poor shot, immediately replace that feeling with another practice swing— "Repeat the good, replace the bad."

IMAGERY PERSPECTIVE

Most good golfers can visualize the flight of the ball they are about to hit, therein reinforcing the target orientation that guides their swing. At the beginning you may picture yourself as if you were in a movie or watching yourself on a videotape. This perspective is called an external view, as if you were watching from the camera's angle (see Figure 12.1a). You will be able to see your entire body, tell what clothes you are wearing, and see your entire swing. As you get better and better, try to imagine yourself from an internal perspective, so that you look down at the top of the club, or from behind the ball (see Figure 12.1b). This is the way you actually see yourself during the swing.

You can enhance your imagery by using videotape. If you have difficulty picturing yourself swing, have someone videotape your swing. Then watch the tape over and over again. By clearly observing your swing, you will develop an image of what you look like as a golfer. Then alternately actually watch one swing and imagine the next swing. This will not only help you imagine various shots, it will also help you build self-confidence (see Step 11).

Watching other great golfers will also aid in your ability to imagine yourself. Watching and analyzing others hit good shots will help you imagine yourself hitting those same shots. The Sybervision tapes that show repeated shots by the same skilled golfer allow you to imagine that same great swing. View the swing from various angles so that you have a good idea of what the swing is really doing.

Imagery can also be effective during practice. While standing on the practice tee, imagine

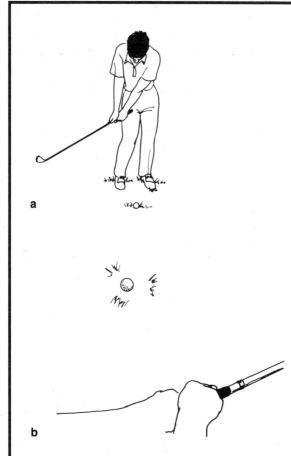

a

b

Figure 12.1 Imagery perspectives: (a) external (as the camera watches you), (b) internal (as you look down at the top of the club and from behind the ball).

various holes of a golf course. Before hitting each shot, imagine a specific target and environment. Once you are able to imagine a particular hole or shot, try playing an entire round in your head. Take a scorecard and play each shot as if you were on a specific hole. If it is a dogleg left, plan your shot as if playing that hole.

Golfers must practice imagery just like they practice other skills. Designate part of your practice for imagery rehearsal that is linked to actual shots. For example, imagine a shot, execute the shot, and then replay the image of that shot. The Keys to Success in Figure 12.2 provide practice checkpoints for using imagery skills effectively.

Figure 12.2 Keys to Success: *Imagery Skills*

In your mind, create a specific situation on the course, or a specific shot. If you are practicing, imagine the shot before each practice swing. If you are playing a round, imagine the shot before each actual attempt.

Visual Imagery

Body: Imagine yourself actually swinging that club

   a. From an external perspective
      (as a camera watches you) ____
   b. From an internal perspective
      (as you look down at the top of the club) ____

Ball: Imagine the desired flight of the ball and its landing at the desired spot or holing out

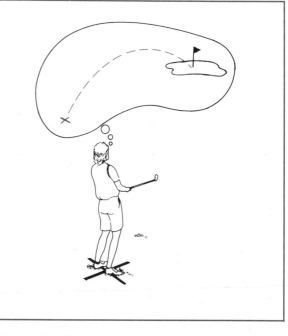

Kinesthetic Imagery

Body: Imagine the feel of the entire swing ____
Hands and arms: Imagine the feel of contacting, then imagine your wrists and hands releasing at the ball ____

Tactile Imagery

Setup: Feel the pressure of your weight on the balls to the instep of your feet
Grip: Feel the grip in your hands

    a. Note the pressure in your middle two fingers of your rear-side hand and in the last three fingers of your target hand ____
    b. Feel the impact of the clubhead on the ball ____

Auditory Imagery

Strike: Hear the club strike the ball ____
Result: Hear the ball land on the target or in the hole ____

Detecting Errors in Imagery

Most imagery errors are errors of omission. Failing to imagine is like imagining to fail. Each time you imagine a shot, you are getting a free practice. It is therefore important to use that free, imaginary shot to simulate the actual shot. Use your routine and feel, see, and hear the desired shot.

ERROR 🚫

CORRECTION

ERROR	CORRECTION
1. Hitting a shot before giving yourself enough time to imagine the desired shot.	1. Build time for imagery into your preshot routine for each shot. Do the imagery at the same spot in your routine each time.
2. Before hitting a shot over water or a sand trap, you visualize the shot landing in the water or sand trap.	2. Use the same ''stoppage'' technique as for thoughts (review Step 11). Then force yourself to seek another, positive image of your shot being successfully executed.
3. Trying to get a ''feeling'' image, but being unable to do so.	3. Take an actual practice swing and focus on the feel of the shot, then imagine that same feel without swinging.

1. Videotape Assistance Drill

Have someone take some videotape footage of your golf swing. Watch your taped swing at least 20 times. Remember that almost everyone is embarrassed, or fails to really see anything, the first few times. As you watch yourself over and over again, you will begin to appreciate your swing. Watch yourself, and then close your eyes and see if you can "replay" your swing. Do not attempt to analyze your swing, just relax and enjoy the image, so that you can internalize it. Try to feel it, see it, and hear it.

Success Goal = Watch yourself swing (on videotape) at least 20 times; then imagine your swing, using as many sensory systems as you can

Your Score = (#) _____ times you watched your swing on videotape and repeated the image in your mind

2. Movie Star Drill

Imagine yourself as if you were on the LPGA/PGA tour and the camera was filming each shot. Picture yourself as if the camera were facing you, filming your entire body and full swing. Then imagine that the camera is in line with the ball and target and filming you from down the line or the rear side. Try to switch the focus in your mind, viewing the same shot from both angles, 10 times.

Success Goal = "Viewing" the same swing from two different angles, being able to switch back and forth in your mind

Your Score = (#) _____ of successful dual viewings in 10 attempts

3. Play a Practice Round in Your Head

From the practice tee, imagine you are playing your favorite golf course. Hit your first ball as if you were standing on the first tee. Then hit the second ball in relation to the imaginary landing of the first ball. That is, if you are playing a par 5 dogleg left, and you hit the first ball straight down the practice tee, hit the second ball toward the left. Each time you hit a ball, imagine that it is the actual shot you would take on that hole. (The good news is that you automatically "make" every putt!)

Success Goal = To be able to imagine each fairway or approach shot in an imaginary 18-hole course; imagine at least 2 shots per hole (at least 36; eliminate the putts because you are on the practice tee area)

Your Score = (#) ____ of shots imagined as if on the actual course

4. Putting Track Drill

At the practice green, imagine each putt as if there were a toy railroad track leading from the ball to the hole. The track should resemble the actual path of the ball (taking into account the green's surface, slope, break, etc.). If you have difficulty doing this, actually draw a chalk line along a carpet to simulate the path. Using an intermediate target will also help.

Success Goal = 20 putts, visualizing the line of the ball's roll for each putt

Your Score = (#) ____ putts visualized and then actually putted

5. Water Hazard Drill

Imagine that you are about to tee off on a par 3 hole, over a big pond, onto a small green. Imagine seeing yourself on the tee watching your ball sail over the water and land near the pin.

Success Goal = Imagine yourself successfully executing a drive across the water; imagine your shot in each of the sensory systems: hear it, feel it, and see it

Your Score = Check the senses in which you imagined the shot

____ hear

____ feel

____ see

6. Imagery Practice During a Round of Golf

Imagery should be part of your preshot routine for every shot and putt you take. Unfortunately, many golfers focus more attention on the physical execution of skills than on the mental concomitants that also influence successful golf performance. To emphasize the importance of imagery, keep track of each shot you hit in 18 holes, and indicate if you used positive images before each shot.

Success Goal = Play 18 holes of golf and create a vivid image for each shot before you execute the shot

Your Score = (#) ____ times you imagined a shot before you hit it in 18 holes, using the following table to help record your imagery (place a checkmark under the club used, and the letter *I* if you imagined)

Hole	1-w	2-w	3-w	5-w	2-i	3-i	4-i	5-i	6-i	7-i	8-i	9-i	PW	SW	Putter
Example	✔*I*	___	___	___	___	___	✔*I*	___	___	___	___	___	✔*I*	___	___
1	___	___	___	___	___	___	___	___	___	___	___	___	___	___	___
2	___	___	___	___	___	___	___	___	___	___	___	___	___	___	___
3	___	___	___	___	___	___	___	___	___	___	___	___	___	___	___
4	___	___	___	___	___	___	___	___	___	___	___	___	___	___	___
5	___	___	___	___	___	___	___	___	___	___	___	___	___	___	___
6	___	___	___	___	___	___	___	___	___	___	___	___	___	___	___
7	___	___	___	___	___	___	___	___	___	___	___	___	___	___	___
8	___	___	___	___	___	___	___	___	___	___	___	___	___	___	___
9	___	___	___	___	___	___	___	___	___	___	___	___	___	___	___
10	___	___	___	___	___	___	___	___	___	___	___	___	___	___	___
11	___	___	___	___	___	___	___	___	___	___	___	___	___	___	___
12	___	___	___	___	___	___	___	___	___	___	___	___	___	___	___
13	___	___	___	___	___	___	___	___	___	___	___	___	___	___	___
14	___	___	___	___	___	___	___	___	___	___	___	___	___	___	___
15	___	___	___	___	___	___	___	___	___	___	___	___	___	___	___
16	___	___	___	___	___	___	___	___	___	___	___	___	___	___	___
17	___	___	___	___	___	___	___	___	___	___	___	___	___	___	___
18	___	___	___	___	___	___	___	___	___	___	___	___	___	___	___

Imagery
Keys to Success Checklist

Imagery is a private matter and must be subject to your own honest evaluation. Excellent golfers are able to imagine in at least one sensory system (not necessarily visual). Use the items in Figure 12.2 as a checklist and evaluate your own ability to effectively imagine yourself hitting a golf shot. Fill out that checklist for your on-course play, too (repeat Drill 6).

Step 13   Strategies for Play

Preparing for a round of golf is as important as practicing the individual skills. You must plan a strategy to manage the course (see Step 10) and deal with the pressures you will face. For each round you play, determine your objective by asking yourself one fundamental question: "Am I playing to practice specific skills that I am trying to learn or change, or am I playing for the outcome (to beat some competitor or score)?" After three rounds, evaluate your play in relation to the strategies you've used, to plan for the next round or practice.

It is also important to consider the environment in which you are playing. Your attitude may be different in a Saturday morning outing with friends than in a tournament round. Playing with your regular competitors will be different from playing with your boss or teacher. The key is to decide ahead of time your objective and needs for that round.

WHY IS IT IMPORTANT TO DETERMINE A STRATEGY EACH TIME YOU PLAY?

Each time you play or practice, you should have a specific goal in mind. Goals will help focus your attention and direct your feelings about the quality of your play. For example, suppose you are trying to make a minor swing change. Often when you're working at changing some aspect of your game, your score will slip, but you must practice the skill to make it a permanent part of your game. So when you play a round, you must decide whether to play through the change or revert to previous habits in order to score. If you go into the round without making a conscious decision, you are likely to have many negative thoughts during play (see Step 11) or end up using a swing that is halfway between the old and the new.

Deciding on the social objective of the round is also important. A frustrating thing for many golfers is to try to mix social and competitive needs. Serious golfers develop the ability to separate social time from the serious moments when shots are hit. It is fine to talk between shots, while you are walking down the fairway—but it is counterproductive if you can-not refocus your attention when you get ready to hit the next shot.

HOW TO PLAN A STRATEGY

Before you go out to play or practice, decide on specific objectives for the day. Are you going to try your new skills and take your chances on making a good score, or are you going to revert to old habits to protect the game you already have? The best golfers are always working on specific skills. They decide ahead of time whether they are going to practice a new skill, and if the answer is yes, they stick to it. If they are making a grip change, they know it will feel uncomfortable at first. They also know that if they give in to the desire to return to old habits, they may temporarily score better, but they will not make much progress toward their real goal.

So you must decide on not only the physical but also the social or business objectives for each session. Are you joining a friend or spouse for some recreation time (and can you commit to the casual conversation that goes with that?), or are you out to work on your game and score as well as possible? Or do you hope to do both? The key is to decide ahead of time and stick with your decision.

Physical Objectives

Many professional golfers talk about the difficulty of "playing through" changes in their game. It is easy to hope to change, but it is difficult to commit to change and stick to a plan for improvement. You must be willing to set goals and delay the gratification of scoring well until the skills are learned or modified. The old adage that "it is easier to learn a new skill than to modify an old habit" is really true. Change requires commitment.

Before playing or practice, decide what you hope to accomplish. Be specific and consider which elements you are working on:

Preswing elements
- Preshot routine
- Grip
- Alignment
- Stance/posture

In-swing elements

- Swing plane
- Release
- Timing/rhythm
- Balance
- Etc.

If you're working on a modified grip, make a commitment to check that you're using the desired grip before each shot. Don't allow yourself to revert to your old habit. Similarly, if you are working on a new ball position or trying to develop a more consistent plane, commit yourself to it on each shot.

Making changes in the mechanics of your golf game requires a continual effort. If you have hit a thousand shots with a weak grip, it will take time to correct that habit. Allowing yourself to revert to the old habit will only reinforce the undesired skill. To prevent this, it's sometimes helpful to identify a "trigger" or reminder for the new skill. For example, a green dot on your golf glove may remind you to check your grip; or tying a yellow ribbon on your shoelaces may remind you to check alignment.

The key is to find some cue or reminder that will help you make the desired change. The alternative is to decide that this is not the right time to practice or test the change. If you are playing in a tournament tomorrow, you may decide to delay the change and rely on old skills. It is better to decide to delay the change than to constantly question yourself during the round. Just decide, and remember that "what-ifs cause whiffs."

Social Objectives

Your golf skills will be tested in many environments: tournament play, play with family or friends, education or business play, and so on.

Each of these situations requires a different mind-set. In a tournament environment, most golfers are serious about scoring well and are generally considerate of others' needs for quiet and concentration. In contrast, social golf with friends often produces idle conversation and many distractions.

Actively deciding on your social strategy will help you focus attention on each shot. It is all right to be sociable and chatty between shots, but if you allow your attention to be distracted before or during the shot, disaster may result. The attentional strategies outlined in Step 11 will help when you are ready to plan and hit the next shot.

The "focus-in" technique is another good strategy to use when playing in a semisocial environment. A round of golf can often take 4 or 5 hours, and it is almost impossible to totally concentrate for that amount of time. Instead, find a cue that refocuses your attention for your shots. Many golfers agree to be social between shots, but when the cart stops, or the bag is set down, they switch to the "attention channel." Imagine watching television. One channel is light humor or comedy, the other is serious sport. Between shots it may be appropriate to switch to the light humor channel and join in the conversation. Then when it is your turn to hit, switch to the serious sport channel. Find a cue that reminds you to switch the channel. For example, each time you stop near your ball, momentarily put your hand on your driver. Or tap the sole of your shoe. Find some behavior that will help your body redirect its attention to the *present* shot.

The Keys to Success in Figure 13.1 will help you prepare and carry out your strategies for play. Commit to your objectives for the round. It will take time to trust your changes, but stick with them.

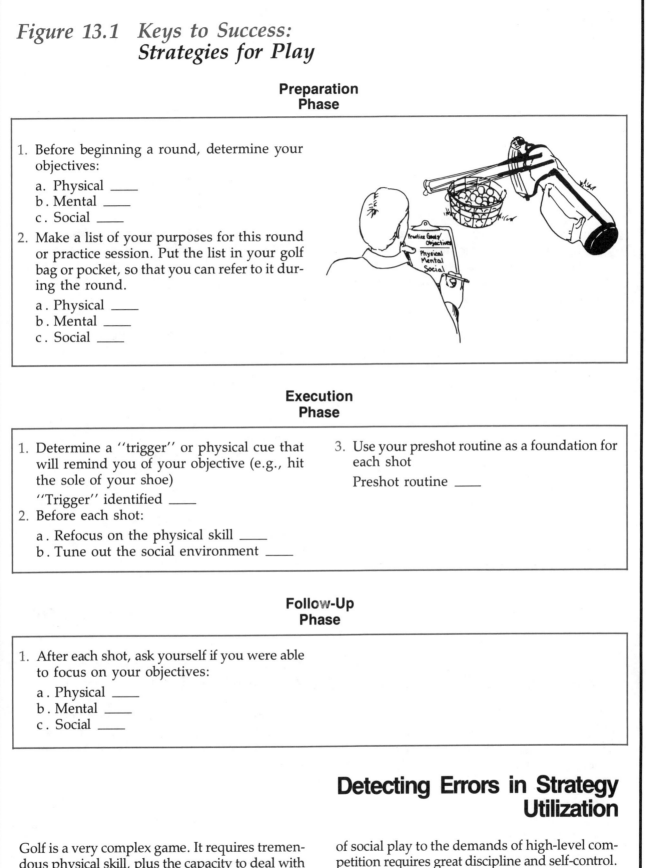

Figure 13.1 Keys to Success: Strategies for Play

Preparation Phase

1. Before beginning a round, determine your objectives:
   a. Physical ____
   b. Mental ____
   c. Social ____
2. Make a list of your purposes for this round or practice session. Put the list in your golf bag or pocket, so that you can refer to it during the round.
   a. Physical ____
   b. Mental ____
   c. Social ____

Execution Phase

1. Determine a "trigger" or physical cue that will remind you of your objective (e.g., hit the sole of your shoe)

   "Trigger" identified ____
2. Before each shot:
   a. Refocus on the physical skill ____
   b. Tune out the social environment ____

3. Use your preshot routine as a foundation for each shot

   Preshot routine ____

Follow-Up Phase

1. After each shot, ask yourself if you were able to focus on your objectives:
   a. Physical ____
   b. Mental ____
   c. Social ____

Detecting Errors in Strategy Utilization

Golf is a very complex game. It requires tremendous physical skill, plus the capacity to deal with the social environment of play. Learning to control your attention and to shift from the demands of social play to the demands of high-level competition requires great discipline and self-control. The following suggestions will help you control your attention.

ERROR 🚫	CORRECTION
1. On the first tee you debate whether to use your new graphite driver (for example) or not.	1. Decide (before you tee off for the day) what skills or clubs you will work on. Once you've made your decision, stick to it.
2. You feel uncomfortable standing over the ball with your new grip (stance, etc.). You hesitate but hit it anyway.	2. If you feel uncomfortable and are having negative thoughts, back away from the shot. Confirm your objective and then reinstitute your preshot routine. *Trust* yourself.
3. Your playing partners are constantly talking about other people, jobs, school, and so on. When you get ready to hit, your mind is racing with thoughts other than golf.	3. Use the thought stoppage technique (Step 11). Remember, it is all right to talk between shots, but at the time of execution you must refocus on the present.
4. The group behind you is pressing. You can't play any faster because of the group ahead of you. You feel rushed on every shot.	4. Evaluate the situation and take control of what you can control. Move quickly between shots, so when it is your turn you are ready. Then take your time, refocus your attention, and use your preshot routine.
5. You have a very busy schedule and many demands on your time. Whenever you get ready to hit, your mind fills with a "to do" list—reminders to pick up one of the children, stop at the bank, etc. Your game is suffering.	5. When you decide to play golf, you have committed to a certain period of time. Leave the other concerns behind. Make a list of things you need to do outside of golf, but leave it in the car or locker. Shed that extra baggage and leave it until later. In the meantime, play each shot, one at a time.

Strategy Drills

1. Determining Objectives for Round of Play Drill

It is essential that you determine your objectives for each round of practice or play. Are you going out to have fun and socialize, practice specific shots, score well, or a combination of these? Each time you go to the practice tee or to play, make a list (either on paper or mentally) of your objectives. This list represents your commitments to yourself for that session.

Success Goal = For at least 10 days, prepare a list of objectives for each day, specifying at least 1 physical and 1 mental/psychological goal

Your Score = (#) ____ days that you prepared a list that includes at least 1 physical and 1 mental/psychological goal

2. Self-Monitoring During Play Drill

After identifying your objectives for the day, monitor your ability to focus on those goals. For each shot you hit, record whether you met those objectives. You can use the following scoresheet. Based on your initial objectives, physical (P) and mental (M), record which were accomplished on each shot. For example, if the physical objective is to check your grip prior to each shot, and the mental/psychological objective is to do a preshot routine before each shot, then place a P and an M for each stroke for which these objectives were accomplished. At the end of the round, determine if you were successful by calculating your percentages for accomplishing your physical and mental/psychological objectives. If you accomplished them better than 80 percent of the time, you need to set higher goals.

Success Goal = For each shot taken during a round of golf, record whether you met your physical (P) and mental/psychological (M) objective on the Self-Monitoring Scoresheet

Self-Monitoring Scoresheet

Today I will work on the following objectives:

Physical objective (P) = _____

Mental/psychological objective (M) = _____

Under each stroke taken, record each objective met by marking either a P or an M (see example below):

Hole number	Par for hole							
		1	**2**	**3**	**4**	**5**	**6**	**7**
Example:	5	M	P, M	P	P	P	P, M	
1								
2								
3								
4								
5								
6								
7								
8								
9								
10								
11								
12								
13								
14								
15								
16								
17								
18								

Number of strokes taken

Your Score =

a. Total number of strokes taken = ____

b. Total number of *P*s marked = ____

c. Total number of *M*s marked = ____

d. $\dfrac{\text{Total number of } Ps}{\text{Total number of strokes taken}}$ = ____ % time met physical goal

e. $\dfrac{\text{Total number of } Ms}{\text{Total number of strokes taken}}$ = ____ % time met mental goal

3. "Oops" (Paper Clip) Self-Monitoring Drill

It is important to monitor your success at accomplishing goals in golf. In Drill 2 you used a scoresheet on which you recorded your success practicing your physical (P) and mental/psychological (M) skills. Unfortunately it is not always convenient to carry a complex scoresheet during play. This drill will show you a way to use paper clips to keep track of your objectives.

Before you begin a practice session or round of golf, identify one physical (P) or one mental/psychological (M) skill you will focus on. Fill one pocket with paper clips. Each time you take a stroke, ask yourself if you met your objective. If you *failed* to complete the objective, move one paper clip from that pocket to an empty pocket, referred to as the "Oops Pocket"—that is, "Oops, I forgot to do my routine [check my grip, etc.]." The ultimate objective is to finish an entire round or practice session and never forget to practice your specified skill. Your Oops Pocket will be empty if you are completely successful.

Success Goal = For each shot taken, meet your P or M objective

Your Score = (%) ____ successful = $\dfrac{\text{\# Paper clips moved}}{\text{Total \# of shots taken}}$

4. Shotkeeper Scorecard Self-Monitoring Drill

Golfers who are serious about getting better, monitor their progress systematically. They often keep track of the physical and mental variables that affect each shot they take. By using a scorecard, you will be able to keep track of the mental and physical skills you need to practice. For example, the following Sample Shotkeeper Scorecard was kept by Tony to help guide his future practice sessions.

On Tony's scorecard, the first shot was a 3-wood on Hole 1. The result was recorded in terms of a physical aspect (above the diagonal line) and a mental aspect (below the diagonal line). He sliced the ball and had excessive body tension. After Tony's round, it was possible to note that he tended to hit slices (and seldom hooks) and forget to use a preshot routine.

In this drill, play 18 holes of golf and carefully record each shot taken on the Shotkeeper Scorecard. Indicate both a physical and a mental weakness (if any) in each shot. When you are finished, summarize your performance by tallying the results for each club used and for the physical and mental behaviors exhibited. For example, how many times did you hit the ball to the right of the target? How often did you have excess body tension or fail to use your routine?

Success Goal = During a round of golf, note at least 1 mental and 1 physical aspect for each shot on the Shotkeeper Scorecard

Sample Shotkeeper Scorecard

Performance Chart

Name: Tony Jones Course: Richmont CC Date: Sept. 9

Hole	Yards	PAR	Woods 1	2	3	4	5	Irons 1	2	3	4	5	6	7	8	9	Wedge	Greens hit in regulation	Putts 1st	2nd	3rd
1	385	4	s BT		s BT							s BT		s BT			— BT		u CC	✓ CC	✓ CC
2	142	3					r FR				r FR						✓ CC		o FR	u FR	✓ CC
3	501	5			r FR		✓ CC					— FR				✓ FR			u BT	✓ CC	✓ BT
4	365	4			s BT		r FR									✓ FR			u BT	o FR	
5	325	4					r FR					✓ FR				✓ FR	— FR		u BT	✓ CC	
6	129	3			s BT							— FR				— FR	✓ FR	✓	u BT	o FR	✓ BT
7	498	5					u FR					— FR		o FR			— FR		u BT	✓ BT	
8	301	4					✓ FR					s BT		o FR		— FR	✓ CC		✓ BT	✓ BT	
9	379	4			s BT		✓ CC					r FR		— FR			— FR		u FR	✓ BT	
10	516	5	s BT				✓ CC					r FR				— FR	✓ CC		o CC	✓ CC	
11	329	4					✓ CC					— FR		— FR			✓ BT		u BT	✓ FR	
12	145	3			s BT						r FR						✓ BT		✓ CC	✓ BT	
13	371	4					✓ CC					— FR				— FR	✓ CC		✓ BT	✓ CC	
14	298	4					✓ CC					r FR					✓ CC		✓ CC	✓ CC	
15	520	5			s BT		✓ CC					r FR				u FR	✓ CC		o FR	✓ CC	
16	318	4	r FR			✓ CC					✓ CC	r FR				u FR	✓ CC	✓	o FR	✓ CC	
17	141	3																	✓ CC		
18	352	4					✓ UA					r BT				u FR	o FR		u FR	✓ CC	

Physical Aspects
✓ = on target
s = sliced
h = hooked
o = beyond target
u = short of target
r = right of target
l = left of target

Mental Aspects
NT = Negative Thinking
LA = Lack of Attentional Control
BT = Excess Body Tension
FR = Failure to use Routine
OA = Overaroused
UA = Underaroused
CC = Complete Mental Control

Summary:

Physical Aspects

✓ = 43	o = 9
s = 9	u = 14
h = 0	r = 12
	l = 11

Mental Aspects

NT = —	OA = —
LA = —	UA = 1
BT = 24	CC = 28
FR = 42	

Note: From Golf: Better Practice for Better Play by L. Bunker & D. Owens, 1984, p. 210. Copyright 1984 by Leisure Press. Adapted by permission.

Shotkeeper Scorecard

Name

Course

Date

Performance Chart

Hole	Yards	PAR	Woods 1	2	3	4	5	Irons 1	2	3	4	5	6	7	8	9	Wedge	Greens hit in regulation	Putts 1st	2nd	3rd
1	385	4																			
2	142	3																			
3	501	5																			
4	365	4																			
5	325	4																			
6	129	3																			
7	498	5																			
8	301	4																			
9	379	4																			
10	516	5																			
11	329	4																			
12	145	3																			
13	371	4																			
14	298	4																			
15	520	5																			
16	318	4																			
17	141	3																			
18	352	4																			

Physical Aspects
✓ = on target
s = sliced
h = hooked
o = beyond target
u = short of target
r = right of target
l = left of target

Mental Aspects
NT = Negative Thinking
LA = Lack of Attentional Control
BT = Excess Body Tension
FR = Failure to use Routine
OA = Overaroused
UA = Underaroused
CC = Complete Mental Control

Summary:

Physical Aspects
✓ =   o =
s =   u =
h =   r =
             l =

Mental Aspects
NT =   OA =
LA =   UA =
BT =   CC =
FR =

Note: From *Golf: Better Practice for Better Play* by L. Bunker & D. Owens, 1984, p. 210. Copyright 1984 by Leisure Press. Adapted by permission.

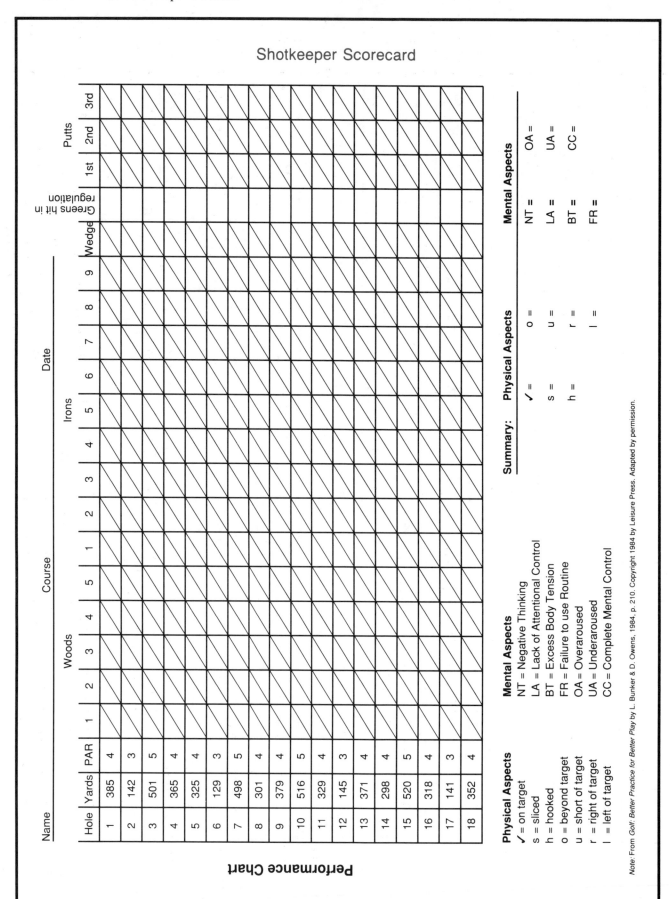

Your Score = Summarize the areas you need to focus on to improve your golf game

Physical Aspects

(#) ____ shots on target (✓)

(#) ____ shots sliced (s)

(#) ____ shots hooked (h)

(#) ____ shots too long (o)

(#) ____ shots too short (u)

(#) ____ shots landing to right of target (r)

(#) ____ shots landing to left of target (l)

Mental Aspects

(#) ____ negative thinking (NT)

(#) ____ lacked attentional control (LA)

(#) ____ excess body tension (BT)

(#) ____ failed to use routine (FR)

(#) ____ overaroused (OA)

(#) ____ underaroused or too relaxed (UA)

(#) ____ complete mental control (CC)

Strategies for Play
Keys to Success Checklist

It is crucial to plan each round of golf. The adage that "failing to plan is planning to fail" certainly pertains to golf. Proficient golfers always determine their overall objective for a round by asking, "Am I playing to practice specific skills, or am I playing for the outcome (to beat some competitor or score)?" Using the checklist in Figure 13.1, evaluate your ability to plan an effective strategy for winning golf.

Step 14 Handicaps and Playing Formats

Competition in golf can be fun and help you develop your game. One of the great advantages of golf is that players of varying skill levels can enjoy playing together. The handicapping system makes it possible to equate players of differing abilities, and the variety of playing formats can allow everyone to contribute to a fun round.

You can test your skills in several types of competitions. The important thing is to decide ahead of time with the people you are playing with what your objectives will be for the outing. Are you playing for the practice or to compete? Will you equate your skills by using the handicapping system, or will you add variety by using one of the various playing formats (e.g., medal play, match play, best ball, nassau, or scramble)?

WHY IS UNDERSTANDING HANDICAPPING AND PLAYING FORMATS IMPORTANT?

All sport experiences involve strategy that enhances your chances for success. The handicapping system allows players of unequal ability to be matched in terms of strokes accumulated. If you want to play social golf, handicaps don't matter. But if you want competition, handicaps can make it more enjoyable—giving, for instance, a player who shoots in the 80s and a player who shoots in the 90s an equitable system in which to compete.

Similarly, each playing format has particular advantages or challenges, depending on your physical and psychological skills. For example, if you tend to focus on short-term goals, match play may be a positive advantage, because each hole is a separate competition. In contrast, medal play is based on a stroke-by-stroke analysis that includes a cumulative evaluation of your play.

HOW TO ESTABLISH A HANDICAP

The United States Golf Association (USGA) has established a system by which players of different abilities can compete on fairly equal grounds. This system is called the USGA Handicap System. Only golf clubs and amateur golf associations authorized by the USGA can issue USGA handicaps.

There are currently two methods of establishing a handicap within the USGA: preslope system and slope system. The preslope system is the original handicapping system; the slope system is a refined version that is now the official USGA handicap system. The slope system takes into consideration the difficulty of the courses on which players play.

Preslope System

The preslope system computes a USGA handicap, which is indicated as a whole number. Figure 14.1 shows a USGA authorized handicap card. The slope system creates a USGA handicap index, which is expressed as a decimal fraction.

OFFICIAL HANDICAP CARD

LAST YEAR HANDICAP 8

NAME JONES, KATHY 1100
CLUB NO. 675 DATE 06/12/91
COG HILL WOMEN'S GOLF AS

COURSE RATING 71.9/118

LAST 20 SCORES
87 82 81* 78* 79*
80* 82* 79* 76* 82
84 85 88 77* 88
79* 86 80 84 78*

GAMES PLAYED THIS YEAR 8

TOTAL DIFF. USED 73.9

8	8	8	7								
1	2	3	4	5	6	7	8	9	10	11	12

HANDICAP PERIODS

SLOPE INDEX 7.1

7

CURRENT HANDICAP

*INDICATES A SCORE USED IN THE COMPUTATION

Figure 14.1 Handicap card. Reprinted by permission.

The computation of a USGA handicap involves a number of variables defined as follows by the USGA:

- *Course rating* is the evaluation of the playing difficulty of a course for scratch players (those who generally score par and have no handicap). It is expressed in strokes and decimal fractions of a stroke and is based on yardage and other obstacles to the extent that they affect a player's scoring ability.
- *Adjusted gross score* is a player's score minus

any adjustments under equitable stroke control. An adjusted score is only used for handicap purposes. (A list of conditions, equitable stroke control, allowable adjustments, and so on can be obtained from the USGA.)

- *Handicap differential* is the difference between a player's adjusted gross score and the USGA course rating for the course on which the score was made.

Example:	Adjusted gross score	98
	USGA course rating	70.5
	Handicap differential	27.5

To establish a handicap, states the *USGA Handicapping Systems Manual*, "the lowest 10 handicap differentials of the last 20 rounds are averaged and multiplied by 96 percent and rounded off to the nearest whole number" (p. 12). The maximum handicap for a man is 36 and for a woman is 40.

Slope System

The slope system computes a USGA handicap index to represent the ability of a player on a course of average difficulty. This system differs from the preslope system in that each course is rated by the USGA based on a variety of factors, to establish a slope rating. The slope ratings go from 84 (least difficult) to 141 (most difficult). Each course has two or three ratings, depending on the number of tees per hole (men's tees and ladies' tees, or red, white, and blue tees as shown in Figure 14.2).

Each course is provided a course handicap table, based on the course slope rating, as illustrated in Figure 14.3. With your established handicap index from your home course, when you go to another golf course to play with friends or in a tournament where your handicap is used, you refer to the course handicap table for that course to determine your course handicap. For example, if your handicap index is 3.9, the course handicap table in Figure 14.3 shows your course handicap to be 4 for that particular course.

The slope system is more involved than the preslope system. However, it is a greater equalizer in tournaments.

To compute the handicap index in the slope system, the adjusted gross score, the USGA course rating, and the difference between the gross score and course rating (previously discussed with the preslope handicap) are used, along with the following:

COG HILL

Course	Rating	Slope	Yards
# 1. (R)	66.6	110	5623
(W)	68.3	114	5989
(B)	69.6	117	6294
# 2. (R)	67.2	111	5755
(W)	68.4	114	6041
(B)	69.4	117	6240
# 3. (R)	65.2	106	5298
(W)	69.1	114	6193
(B)	70.1	117	6437
# 4. (R)	76.7	134	5874
(W)	71.8	138	6366
(B)	75.6	142	6992

TEE KEY

(R) = Red   (W) = White   (B) = Blue

Form 1499

COG HILL GOLF and COUNTRY CLUB

Tee Times by Phone,
Six (6) days in advance.
CALL –

COG HILL 708-257-5872
    Chicago line . . 312-242-1717

ST. ANDREWS . . 708-287-7775
    Chicago line . . 312-231-3100

PINE MEADOW. .708-566-GOLF

GLENWOODIE . . 708-758-1212

Figure 14.2   Rating examples of course, slope, and yardage. Reprinted by permission.

Slope Rating

USGA Handicap	Course index hdcp	USGA Handicap	Course index hdcp
+2.6 to +1.6	+2	24.0 to 25.0	23
+1.5 to +.6	+1	25.1 to 26.1	24
+.5 to .5	0	26.2 to 27.1	25
0.6 to 1.5	1	27.2 to 28.2	26
1.6 to 2.6	2	28.3 to 29.3	27
2.7 to 3.7	3	29.4 to 30.3	28
3.8 to 4.7	4	30.4 to 31.4	29
4.8 to 5.8	5	31.5 to 32.5	30
5.9 to 6.9	6	32.6 to 33.5	31
7.0 to 7.9	7	33.6 to 34.6	32
8.0 to 9.0	8	34.7 to 35.7	33
9.1 to 10.1	9	35.8 to 36.4	34
10.2 to 11.1	10		
11.2 to 12.2	11		
12.3 to 13.3	12		
13.4 to 14.3	13		
14.4 to 15.4	14		
15.5 to 16.5	15		
16.6 to 17.5	16		
17.6 to 18.6	17		
18.7 to 19.7	18		
19.8 to 20.7	19		
20.8 to 21.8	20		
21.9 to 22.9	21		
23.0 to 23.9	22		

Figure 14.3 Sample course handicap table.

- A *handicap differential* is the difference between a player's adjusted gross score and the USGA course rating of the course on which the score was made, multiplied by 113, then divided by the slope rating of the course.
- *Slope rating* reflects the relative playing difficulty of a course for players with handicaps *above* scratch.

Example: Here is a computation of a slope handicap differential:

Slope rating of course	120
Adjusted gross score	98
USGA course rating	70.5
Difference	27.5

$$\text{Handicap differential} = \frac{113 \times 27.5}{120} = 25.9$$

According to the *USGA Handicapping System Manual* (p. 10), to establish a USGA handicap index, "total the lowest 10 handicap differentials and multiply the result by .096. Do not round off to the nearest tenth."

The following example shows the contrast between computing handicaps using the preslope versus the slope method.

Example: Slope versus preslope method for handicap calculations:

	Preslope System	Slope System
Adjusted gross score	98	98
USGA course rating	70.5	70.5
Handicap differential	27.5	$\dfrac{113 \times 27.5}{25.9} =$

Handicap:

Lowest 10 differentials of last 20 rounds, averaged and multiplied by 96 percent. Round to nearest whole = 28.

Handicap index:

Lowest 10 handicap differentials totaled and multiplied by .096.

HOW TO USE YOUR HANDICAP

A handicap can be applied to the total strokes for a round, or hole by hole. For the hole-by-hole method, each hole on a golf course is rated in terms of its difficulty and assigned a handicap number (see the scorecard in Figure 10.1). For example, the 2nd hole may be judged the most difficult, in which case the scorecard will list it as the #1 handicap hole, and if you have a handicap, you get a stroke on that hole. If you have a handicap of 15, you would get a stroke on each hole rated 1 through 15, but not on holes rated 16 through 18.

If your handicap is greater than 18, you will get more than one stroke on some holes. For example, if your handicap is 22, you will get one stroke for each of the 18 holes, plus an additional stroke each on the holes rated 1 through 4.

HOW TO PLAY UNDER VARIOUS COMPETITIVE SITUATIONS

There are many different competitive styles of golf. Most common types include match (direct competition) versus medal (stroke) play, scrambles, best balls, and nassaus.

Match Versus Medal Play

The two main forms of competitive golf are match play and medal or stroke play. In match play, the person with the fewest strokes on a hole wins that hole, and the competitor who wins the most holes in a round of 18 holes is the winner. If the match is even after 18 holes, play continues until one player wins a hole. In contrast, in medal or stroke play, the competitor with the lowest number of strokes for 18 holes is the winner.

Medal or stroke play is the format for most competitive tournaments. A tournament may last 1 day or longer, usually not more than 4 days. PGA (Professional Golf Association) and LPGA (Ladies Professional Golf Association) tournaments are usually 4 days. The scores for each day are totaled, and the player with the lowest total

score for the 4 days is the winner. If there are many players, the lowest scores after 2 days may be used to "cut" the field to a smaller number of competitors for the final 2 days.

Match play is typically used for most USGA amateur tournaments. This is an elimination format usually requiring more than 4 days. Players typically compete for 2 days in a medal play format, after which their scores are totaled and players are eliminated to decrease the field to a predetermined number of competitors.

Players are then rank-ordered in two groups, A and B, and paired for competition. Match winners from group A are then paired against match winners from group B, and the losers are eliminated from the tournament. This format continues until one player remains undefeated as the winner of the tournament.

In match play, you compete hole by hole rather than by total score. If you win the first hole, you are said to be one up. If you have won five holes, and your opponent has won three holes, you are two up, and so on. Toward the end of the round, if you are behind more holes than there are holes left to play, your opponent is declared the winner. For example, in tournament play, if your opponent is three up with two holes left, there is no reason to continue to play, and your opponent will be declared the winner, 3:2.

Both match and medal formats can be fun. Some players prefer one format over the other. A player who has high scores on two or three holes and fairly good scores on the rest may enjoy match play, because in this format two or three high-score holes can be less costly than in overall stroke play. Each hole is essentially a new competition, compared with medal play, where the score is cumulative.

Your handicap is used differently in match and medal play. In medal play, your handicap comes off of the final gross score. If you have a handicap of 10 and shot an 88, your net score would be 78. If you are competing with another person, determine the difference between your handicaps before teeing off on the first hole. At the end of the round, subtract the difference between the two players' handicaps from the weaker player's gross score. For example, if your handicap is 10 and your opponent's is 4, you would subtract 6 strokes from your gross score (88) for a net of 82. (If you are competing with more than one golfer, all players subtract their handicaps from their own gross score.) In match play, you must deal with the handicap on each hole. In the preceding example, you would get one stroke on the holes with handicap ratings 1 through 6.

Scramble

A scramble format (or "captains choice," as it is often called) is unique in that you do not play your own ball on each shot. This is a team event that's used as a tournament format as well as for social enjoyment. The number of players per team may vary from 2 to 5 or more. Each player hits a tee shot. Then the best shot is selected by the team. All the players now hit their own balls from where that best shot lies. This selection process is continued until the ball is holed out.

This format is fun because players of all abilities can play together. Everyone has an opportunity to contribute. Even the weakest player will have a great shot or two that can be selected by the team—a very gratifying experience!

Best Ball

A best ball event is also a team event. It is used in social games among friends and in tournament settings. The team can be two players or four players. In this event the lowest individual score of the team on each hole is counted. Each player plays her or his own ball throughout the round, but only the best score for each hole is counted. If the team is four players, two scores are often counted rather than one.

Nassau

In the nassau format the competition can be individual or team and either match or medal format. The players determine this before they begin. Scoring is different in this format. The nassau has a 3-point scoring system, 1 point for the front nine (Holes 1 through 9), 1 point for the back nine (Holes 10 through 18), and 1 point for winning the overall greater number of holes. Let us assume that players A and B are competitors in a match play event. They scored the following:

Front Nine: (Holes 1-9)	Player A wins 6 holes
	Player B wins 3 holes
	Player A receives 1 point, winning by 3 holes, or three up.
Back Nine: (Holes 10-18)	Player A wins 3 holes
	Player B wins 5 holes
	Players A and B tie one hole
	Player B wins 1 point winning 2 holes, or two up
Total:	Player A wins 9 holes (6 + 3)
	Player B wins 8 holes (3 + 5)
	Player A wins 1 point winning by 1 hole, or one up
	Nassau winner = Player A with 2 points (sum of front nine and total)

If there is a tie, no points are awarded.

The nassau format is like having three competitions in one 18-hole round. It can be very exciting and highly competitive in team play.

Playing Format Drills

1. Medal Play Drill

On a regulation golf course, play 18 holes of golf, recording your score for each hole. If you have a handicap, deduct the strokes from the appropriate holes.

Success Goal = Accurately keeping your score for 18 holes and deducting the appropriate strokes for your handicap (if you do not have a handicap at this point, assume that your handicap is 15, and score your round accordingly)

Your Score =

a. (#) ＿＿ actual strokes taken

b. (#) ＿＿ adjusted score, applying your handicap

2. Match Play Drill

In pairs, play a round of golf using the match play format. After each hole, record your score and determine who won that hole. Keep track of the number of "holes up" as you go along. Determine the winner at the end. Assume you are both scratch players.

Success Goal = Accurately keeping your match score on a hole-by-hole basis

Hole number	Player A's score	Player B's score	Hole number	Player A's score	Player B's score
1	＿＿	＿＿	10	＿＿	＿＿
2	＿＿	＿＿	11	＿＿	＿＿
3	＿＿	＿＿	12	＿＿	＿＿
4	＿＿	＿＿	13	＿＿	＿＿
5	＿＿	＿＿	14	＿＿	＿＿
6	＿＿	＿＿	15	＿＿	＿＿
7	＿＿	＿＿	16	＿＿	＿＿
8	＿＿	＿＿	17	＿＿	＿＿
9	＿＿	＿＿	18	＿＿	＿＿

Your Score =

(#) ＿＿ holes won (circle the score for the hole winner from each hole)

3. Nassau Play Drill

Using the scores from Drill 2, convert your scores to a nassau system. That is, determine a winner for the front nine, back nine, and total.

Success Goal = Accurately determining your scores for the nassau format

Your Score =

a. (#) ____ points (1 or 0) won from front 9

b. (#) ____ points (1 or 0) won from back 9

c. (#) ____ points (1 or 0) won for the total 18 holes

4. Determining Your Handicap Index Drill

The handicapping system in golf is an advantage to all golfers, because it allows golfers of all ability levels to compete together on more equal terms. Determine your handicap index, supposing you shot 10 rounds of golf with the following adjusted scores: 120, 100, 98, 105, 97, 100, 94, 95, 98, and 97. The course rating is 72.6, and the slope rating is 126. Round your figures to the nearest 10th.

If possible, actually play 10 rounds of golf and determine your own handicap. If you play only 9 holes at a time, not 18, simply double the score for each round. After you have once determined your handicap, update it by always using the 10 best rounds out of the last 20 rounds you played.

Success Goal = Determine handicaps (a) for the imagined scores given, and (b) for your actual scores after playing 10 rounds of golf; then check your method of calculation by referring to the description of the slope handicapping system.

Your Score =

a. (#) ____ handicap index with imaginary scores (see answer at the end of this step)

b. (#) ____ your own real handicap index

5. Golf Lotto Drill

One of the most important mental skills of golf is the ability to "stay in the present" and play only one shot and hole at a time. The Golf Lotto Drill is designed to emphasize the fact that each hole is important in itself.

Play 18 holes of regulation golf with a friend. Afterward, write the numbers 1 through 18 on small slips of paper and put them in a cup or hat. To determine your score for 9 holes, draw 9 numbers out of the hat. Each represents a hole you have already played and will be used to determine your score. For example, if you drew the numbers 2, 9, 17, 12, 8, 5, 7, 4, 13, add your score for each of those holes to determine your 9 hole score. The best golfer has the lowest 9-hole score using only the holes that were drawn.

Success Goal = Play the Golf Lotto Drill with a friend

Your Score = (#) ____ strokes for 9 holes as drawn by lot

6. Point Game Drill

This is a fun game in which the score is not important. Having the lowest number of strokes does not make you the winner. The objective is to score the most points using the following system:

- 1 point for hitting the fairway
- 1 point for hitting the green
- 1 point for a one putt
- 2 points for no putts
- 2 points for an up-and-down out of the trap ("sandy") or off the green
- −1 point for a 3-putt
- For a birdie, double your points for the hole and wipe out the other players' points on the hole
- For an eagle, triple your points and wipe out the other players' points on the hole

If more than one player gets a birdie or eagle, they tie and wipe out the other players' points.

Success Goal = Play the Point Game Drill with a friend

Your Score = (#) _____ points earned

Answer to Drill 4

Determining Handicap Index

Score	−	Course Rating	=	Differential	× 113	=	Product	÷	Slope Index	=	Handicap Index
120	−	72.6	=	47.4	× 113	=	5356.2	÷	126	=	42.51
100	−	72.6	=	27.4	× 113	=	3096.2	÷	126	=	24.57
98	−	72.6	=	25.4	× 113	=	2870.2	÷	126	=	22.78
105	−	72.6	=	32.4	× 113	=	3661.2	÷	126	=	29.06
97	−	72.6	=	24.4	× 113	=	2757.2	÷	126	=	21.88
100	−	72.6	=	27.4	× 113	=	3096.2	÷	126	=	24.57
94	−	72.6	=	21.4	× 113	=	2418.2	÷	126	=	19.19
95	−	72.6	=	22.4	× 113	=	2531.2	÷	126	=	20.09
98	−	72.6	=	25.4	× 113	=	2870.2	÷	126	=	22.78
97	−	72.6	=	24.4	× 113	=	2757.2	÷	126	=	21.88

Total = 249.31
× .096
Handicap Index 23.93376
or
23.9
(rounded)

Rating Your Progress

Many specific skills must be mastered to lower your handicap and improve your enjoyment of golf. The following is a list of the skills and techniques you should have mastered through using this book. Please rate yourself in each category.

	Very Successful	Fairly Successful	Partially Successful	Unsuccessful
Physical Skills				
Setup (consistency)				
Grip	——	——	——	——
Alignment	——	——	——	——
Basic full swing				
With irons	——	——	——	——
With woods	——	——	——	——
Spin control				
Draw	——	——	——	——
Fade	——	——	——	——
Trajectory control				
High	——	——	——	——
Low	——	——	——	——
Chipping				
Normal	——	——	——	——
Off-green putting	——	——	——	——
Pitching				
Lob	——	——	——	——
Basic	——	——	——	——
Pitch and run	——	——	——	——
Putting	——	——	——	——
Sand				
Explosion shot (high trajectory)	——	——	——	——
Buried lie (low trajectory)	——	——	——	——
Fairway bunkers	——	——	——	——
Challenge shots				
Knees shot	——	——	——	——
Tree shot	——	——	——	——
Backward shot	——	——	——	——

	Very Successful	Fairly Successful	Partially Successful	Unsuccessful
Understanding the Environment				
Reading greens				
Slope	____	____	____	____
Grain of grass	____	____	____	____
Playing in the Environment				
Rain	____	____	____	____
Hot	____	____	____	____
Cold	____	____	____	____
Wind	____	____	____	____
Course Management				
Plotting strategy	____	____	____	____
Psychological Skills				
Positive thinking	____	____	____	____
Thought stoppage	____	____	____	____
Affirmations	____	____	____	____
Imagery				
Internal perspective	____	____	____	____
External perspective	____	____	____	____
Handicaps				
Calculated by slope method	____	____	____	____
Calculated by preslope method	____	____	____	____
Playing Formats				
(Understand and have played)				
Stroke (Medal)	____	____	____	____
Match	____	____	____	____
Scramble	____	____	____	____
Best ball	____	____	____	____
Nassau	____	____	____	____

After you have rated your golf progress, review the areas that you have rated "partially successful" and "unsuccessful." List those skills in the space provided:

My skill areas for future concentrated practice

These skills should make up at least 75% of your future practice time. Consider reviewing the steps that govern those skills, and practice the drills. When you set your practice objectives, focus on the areas where you need to improve. Don't ignore the areas where you already feel confident, but try not to spend more than 25% of your practice time on them.

SUMMARY

The *steps to success* we have described were designed to provide you with a systematic way to improve your game and lower your handicap. There are no magic tricks—just good basic fundamentals for effective golf. Try to practice the skills and drills in the order presented within each step. If you have difficulty with a drill, go back to the preceding one to check on your foundation skills. Then move on to more challenging skills and techniques!

Appendix A Clubs That Can Change Your Game

The equipment market is extensive. If you browse through golf magazines or golf shops, you can see a mind-boggling selection of equipment that varies widely in cost, appearance, weight, length, and use. The unknowing consumer is at the mercy of the salesperson. Before you go running out for the latest in equipment, get an idea of what you need. This section will provide you with some guidelines.

WHAT CLUBS ARE IMPORTANT FOR ADVANCED PLAYERS?

A full set of clubs is not usually recommended for beginning golfers, because it provides too many choices and creates confusion. As your game has improved, your swing technique has become more consistent, as have your swing tempo and speed. Now you can begin to focus on greater precision in distance and directional control. A full set of clubs will add depth to your game. Specialty clubs also take on greater meaning as your skill improves. Wedges and putters are important scoring clubs, and finding the right ones can make a difference.

SELECTION CONSIDERATIONS

Manufacturers are designing clubs with the individual golfer in mind, rather than on the theory that one model fits all. In selecting your equipment, you need to be sure the club fits you in length, lie, weight, shaft flex, and grip size. The length and lie of the club are determined by your physical height and address position as you set up to the ball. Weight and shaft flex are determined by your physical strength and clubhead speed.

As progressive as most manufacturers are today, they are still in the dark ages in labeling equipment by sex (''men's'' and ''women's''). This type of labeling often prevents the proper selection of equipment to fit the individual. Many women need longer and heavier equipment labeled ''men's,'' just as many men need shorter and lighter equipment labeled ''women's.'' In selecting your equipment, ignore the label and find the equipment that fits *you*.

Length

Correct club length is based on your height and swing posture. There are no guidelines matching specific heights with specific club lengths. A major reason for this is arm length, which must be evaluated in conjunction with your swing posture. Many individuals have exceptionally long or short arms for their height. This affects fit for club length and lie, which will be discussed later. The following are *general* guidelines to provide you with a starting point in assessing your needs in club length:

- 4 feet to 5 feet, 3 inches: Junior/women's petite
- 5 feet, 4 inches to 5 feet, 7 inches: Women's standard
- 5 feet, 8 inches to 6 feet, 2 inches: Men's standard
- 6 feet, 3 inches and taller: Extra length and/or lie adjustments

Lie

The *lie* of the club is the position of the sole of the club as it rests on the ground in your address position. Figure A.1, a-c, illustrates the three possible positions of the club at address. Note that in the desired lie position (a), the sole of the club is flat to the ground. A club lie that is too flat (c) has the heel of the club elevated, and one that is too upright (b) has the toe of the club elevated. The lie of the club affects both the potential distance and the direction of your ball flight. The desired lie provides for the most effective club-ball contact. In the other two positions, contact is off-center, causing combinations of distance and directional errors. The most commonly observed directional errors when the club toe is elevated are thin shots to the right, for the right-handed player. When

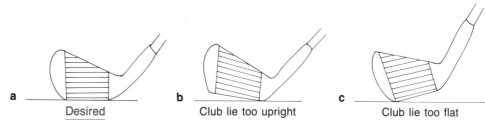

Figure A.1   Club lies.

the heel of the club is elevated, shots tend to be pulled to the left, for the right-handed player, and create deep divots. Be sure to have the lie fit *your* height and posture.

Weight

Club weight is measured in two ways, as swing weight and as overall weight. *Swing weight* is the club's weight distribution from the head of the club to the grip. A swing-weight scale is used to assess this, with values that range from A to E (i.e., light to heavy). Most clubs are in the C to D range.

The *overall weight* of the club is measured in ounces. This is not as commonly used as swing weight. However, there is a noticeable difference in the overall weight of clubs now, with the variety of shafts available. The more commonly used shaft is steel, which is heavier than the more expensive graphite and titanium shafts.

A club that is either too heavy or too light for you can impair your ability to create optimum club-head speed. As with length, there are only general guidelines for club weight. These use the swing-weight measures. The guidelines that follow are based on the individual's arm and hand strength and swing speed.

- C1-C4: Women's lightweight
- C5-C7: Women's standard
- C7-C9: Stronger women, men's lightweight
- D0-D3: Men's standard
- D4-up: Men's extra heavy

These descriptions are based on the traditional assumption that all women are less strong than all men. In fact, many strong women with good clubhead speed play with men's clubs (D weights). You should try a variety of clubs and consult a club-fitting expert to select the best weight.

Shaft Flex

Shaft flex is determined by your strength and swing speed and ranges from flexible to stiff. A weaker player with a slower swing speed may perform better with a more flexible shaft, which helps to create a little more clubhead speed. The stronger player who already creates a fast clubhead speed and is experiencing directional control that does not seem to be technique related may benefit from a stiffer shaft to gain greater clubhead control. Most players fall in the ''regular'' shaft range. There is often an assumption by better players that they need a stiff shaft. This is unwarranted, as not every player has the physical strength and swing speed to accommodate the stiff shaft.

Grip Size

Grip size is a *very* important factor in the proper fit of your equipment. However, your grip size can be adjusted once the other factors are determined and the clubs are selected. You should inquire at the place of purchase if grip adjustments are included in the price of the clubs or if they cost extra. Many golf shops include this in the cost of the equipment.

Your grip size is determined by your hand size. In the recommended fit, the middle finger of your target hand just touches the palm. Figure A.2, a-c, illustrates the desired grip size (b) and grip sizes that are too small (a) and too large (c). The desired fit maximizes your hand action and ability to control the club. If you are taking golf instruction, your teacher or coach may recommend a modification in grip size for your specific swing needs.

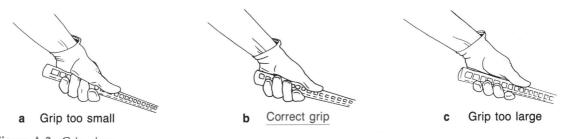

| a   Grip too small | b   Correct grip | c   Grip too large |

Figure A.2   Grip sizes.

SPECIALTY CLUBS

Wedges and putters are usually considered specialty clubs. Players search a long time before finding wedges and putters they really like. These are important clubs for scoring. Most good players believe that saving shots around the greens is more important than hitting the longest drives. This is a difficult concept for the average player to understand, but an important one to becoming a good player.

Wedges

The three-wedge system is popular among low-handicap players. This provides greater variability in the short-game shots. As your play improves, you will need a pitch shot that is shorter, higher, and softer. This is a difficult shot for many players with a sand wedge or pitching wedge, because of the swing changes necessary to create the high, soft ball flight. Under pressure, the fewer adjustments needed, the better! The "third wedge" has more loft than the basic sand wedge—about 60 to 65 degrees of loft, compared to the sand wedge's 56 to 59 degrees. The additional loft provides height and softness with fewer adjustments in your swing. It's not a club for everyone. Usually another club must be eliminated to carry the third wedge, given the 14-club limit.

Putters

Confidence in putting comes from a variety of sources other than just technique. Players select putters based on many factors, among which are appearance, design, weight, and feel. To many players the putter has to look good to them as they address the ball. Some prefer bold straight lines; others prefer a softer, round appearance. Some prefer putters that have lines for alignment; others prefer no lines. There is a great array of appearances to select from (see Figure A.3, a-c).

Figure A.3   Putter designs.

The designs of putter blades also vary. Blades range from very thin to wide. The shaft can be located anywhere from one end of the putter blade to the other. Shaft length varies from short to long, particularly with the advent of the long putters.

The weight and feel of a putter usually go together. Some players have two putters of the same design that differ in weight. They select the putter that best matches the speed of the greens and their stroke feel. On slow greens a lighter putter requires a firmer stroke, whereas on fast greens the stroke needs to be solid, but delicate. The player's feel is the key to her or his putter choice.

SUMMARY

Equipment is a big investment. Take time to explore your options. Whenever possible, try different clubs before making your final decision. Talk to other players, teaching professionals, and knowledgeable salespersons. Be sure the equipment fits your game and your specific fitting needs. Don't make your game fit the equipment.

Shotkeeper Scorecard

Name _____ Course _____ Date _____

Performance Chart

Hole	Yards	PAR	Woods 1	2	3	4	5	Irons 1	2	3	4	5	6	7	8	9	Wedge	Greens hit in Regulation	Putts 1st	2nd	3rd
1																					
2																					
3																					
4																					
5																					
6																					
7																					
8																					
9																					
10																					
11																					
12																					
13																					
14																					
15																					
16																					
17																					
18																					

Physical Aspects
✓ = on target
s = sliced
h = hooked
o = beyond target
u = short of target
r = right of target
l = left of target

Mental Aspects
NT = Negative Thinking
LA = Lack of Attentional Control
BT = Excess Body Tension
FR = Failure to use Routine
OA = Overaroused
UA = Underaroused
CC = Complete Mental Control

Summary: Physical Aspects

✓ =   o =
s =   u =
h =   r =
             l =

Mental Aspects

NT =   OA =
LA =   UA =
BT =   CC =
FR =

Suggested Readings

Alter, M.J. (1990). *Sport stretch*. Champaign, IL: Leisure Press.

Baechle, T.R., & Groves, B.R. (1992). *Weight training: Steps to success*. Champaign, IL: Leisure Press.

Bunker, L.K., & Owens, D. (1984). *Golf: Better practice for better play*. Champaign, IL: Leisure Press.

Croce, P. (1984). *Stretching for athletics*. Champaign, IL: Leisure Press.

Harris, D.V., & Harris, B.L. (1984). *The athlete's guide to sports psychology: Mental skills for physical people*. Champaign, IL: Human Kinetics.

Jobe, F.W., & Schwaab, D.R. (1986). *Thirty exercises for better golf*. Inglewood, CA: Champion Press.

Owens, D. (Ed.) (1984). *Golf for special populations*. Champaign, IL: Leisure Press.

Owens, D., & Bunker, L.K. (1989). *Golf: Steps to success*. Champaign, IL: Leisure Press.

Owens, D., & Bunker, L.K. (1989). *Teaching golf: Steps to success*. Champaign, IL: Leisure Press.

Owens, D., & Bunker, L.K. (1989). *Coaching golf effectively*. Champaign, IL: Leisure Press.

Rotella, R.J., & Bunker, L.K. (1981). *Mind mastery for winning golf*. Englewood Cliffs, NJ: Prentice Hall.

Wiren, G. (1976, April). The search for the perfect teaching method. *National Golf Foundation Information Sheet*, **25**(7): 1-5.

Yocum, L.A., & Mottram, R. (1988). *Women's exercise guide to better golf*. Inglewood, CA: Champion Press.

About the Authors

DeDe Owens, EdD, is the head teaching professional at Cog Hill Golf Club in Lemont, Illinois, and a member of *Golf Digest's* instructional staff. A former professional on the Ladies Professional Golf Association tour, she holds the LPGA Master Teacher ranking and was cited as their Teacher of the Year in 1978. She was also named teacher of the Year by the midwest section of the LPGA each year from 1988 to 1991.

In 1986, Dr. Owens received the Joe Graffis Award from the National Golf Foundation for her "outstanding contribution to golf education." This contribution has been made through both her work as a club professional and her teaching at the University of North Carolina, Delta State University, Illinois State University, and the University of Virginia. Dr. Owens has also made presentations in the Netherlands and Switzerland for the European PGA. She is the editor of *Teaching Golf to Special Populations* and coauthor of *Golf: Steps to Success, Teaching Golf: Steps to Success, Coaching Golf Effectively,* and *Golf: Better Practice for Better Play*, all published by Leisure Press.

Linda K. Bunker, PhD, is a sport psychologist and the associate dean for academic and student affairs at the University of Virginia. She is a consultant for both the National Golf Foundation and the LPGA and is on the advisory boards of the Women's Sport Foundation and the Melpomene Institute, the Minneapolis-based research institute for women in sport.

Dr. Bunker has provided golf workshops for PGA professionals from Japan, the Netherlands, and the United States. Widely published, she is the coauthor of many books, including *Mind Mastery for Winning Golf; Mind, Set and Match; Sport Psychology: Maximizing Sport Potential; Parenting Your Superstar; Golf: Steps to Success; Teaching Golf: Steps to Success;* and *Golf: Better Practice for Better Play*. A former nationally ranked junior tennis player, Dr. Bunker remains an avid tennis player when she is not on the links.